The BIG PENNSYLVANIA REPRODUCIBLE Activity Book!

BY CAROLE MARSH

This activity book has material which correlates with Pennsylvania's Academic Standards.

At every opportunity, we have tried to relate information to the History and Social Science, English, Science, Math, Civics, Economics, and Computer Technology Pennsylvania PAS directives.

For additional information, go to our websites: **www.pennsylvaniaexperience.com** or **www.gallopade.com.**

Correlates with the Pennsylvania PAS Academic Standards

Published by

GALL**O**PADE™ INTERNATIONAL

800-536-2GET
www.gallopade.com

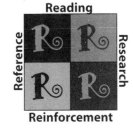

Reading
Reference **R R** Research
R R
Reinforcement

NSSEA

A Word From The Author

Pennsylvania is a very special state. Almost everything about Pennsylvania is interesting and fun! It has a remarkable history that helped create the great nation of America. Pennsylvania enjoys an amazing geography of incredible beauty and fascination. The state's people are unique and have accomplished many great things.

This Activity Book is chock-ful of activities to entice you to learn more about Pennsylvania. While completing mazes, dot-to-dots, word searches, coloring activities, word codes, and other fun-to-do activities, you'll learn about Pennsylvania's history, geography, people, places, animals, legends, and more.

Whether you're sitting in a classroom, stuck inside on a rainy day, or—better yet—sitting in the back seat of a car touring the wonderful state of Pennsylvania, my hope is that you have as much fun using this Activity Book as I did writing it.

Enjoy your Pennsylvania Experience—it's the trip of a lifetime!!

Carole Marsh

©2003 Carole Marsh/Gallopade International/800-536-2GET/www.pennsylvaniaexperience.com/Page 2

The Pennsylvania Experience Series

The Pennsylvania Experience! Paperback Book

My First Pocket Guide to Pennsylvania!

The Big Pennsylvania Reproducible Activity Book

The Pennsylvania Coloring Book!

My First Book About Pennsylvania!

Pennsylvania Jeopardy: Answers and Questions About Our State

Pennsylvania "Jography!": A Fun Run Through Our State

The Pennsylvania Experience! Sticker Pack

The Pennsylvania Experience! Poster/Map

Discover Pennsylvania CD-ROM

Pennsylvania "GEO" Bingo Game

Pennsylvania "HISTO" Bingo Game

Color Me!

BROWN
Like the White-tailed Deer
Brown

BLUE
Like the Pennsylvania sky
Blue

BLACK
Like the stripes of the honeybee
Black

YELLOW
Like ripe corn on the cob
Yellow

PURPLE
Like the native violet
Purple

RED
Like a Pennsylvania sunset
Red

GREEN
Like the leaves of the Mountain Laurel
Green

ORANGE
Like autumn leaves
Orange

©2003 Carole Marsh/Gallopade International/800-536-2GET/www.pennsylvaniaexperience.com/Page 4

Our State Bird!

Connect the dots to see Pennsylvania's beautiful state bird, the Ruffed Grouse.

When you are done, color the bird.

Write the bird's name in the space below.

Ruffed Grouse like to eat leaves, buds, and fruits of forest plants.

Ruffed Grouse look a lot like brown chickens.

1.

26.

18.

2.

25.

19.   17.

3.

24.

20.   16.

23.

21.   15.

4.

13.   14.

12.

5.   22.

11.

10.

They lay cream-colored eggs.

6.

9.

7.

8.

They build their nests on the ground, and line them with leaves.

___ ___ ___ ___ ___ ___   ___ ___ ___ ___ ___ ___

©2003 Carole Marsh/Gallopade International/800-536-2GET/www.pennsylvaniaexperience.com/Page 5

Benjamin Franklin

Benjamin Franklin was born in Boston, Massachusetts in 1706. He moved to Philadelphia when he was 17 and made himself famous as a writer, scientist, and public servant. Franklin published his own paper, the *Pennsylvania Gazette,* and wrote a book of funny and wise sayings called *Poor Richard's Almanack.*

Franklin was a curious man, and he experimented during thunderstorms until he invented the lightning rod. He also invented bifocal glasses and the Franklin stove. Franklin signed the Declaration of Independence and several other important documents. Benjamin Franklin was certainly a well-rounded man!

Answer the following questions:

1. Where was Benjamin Franklin born? _____

2. When did he move to Philadelphia? _____

3. What was the name of his newspaper? _____

4. Name two things that he invented. _____ _____

5. What is one document that he signed? _____

_____

ANSWERS: 1. Boston 2. when he was 17 OR 1723 3. *Pennsylvania Gazette* 4. bifocal glasses, the Franklin stove, the lightning rod 5. the Declaration of Independence

Local Government

Pennsylvania's state government, just like our national government, is made up of three branches. Each branch has a certain job to do. Each branch also has some power over the other branches. We call this system checks and balances. The three branches work together to make our government run smoothly.

Match each of the professionals with their branch.

This branch is made up of the General Assembly which has two houses, the Senate and the House of Representatives. This branch makes and repeals laws.	This branch includes the government leaders made up of the governor, as well as appointed and elected state officials. This branch makes sure that the laws are enforced.	This branch includes the court system, which consists of the local, district, and state courts. This branch interprets the laws.
A. Legislative Branch	**B. Executive Branch**	**C. Judicial Branch**

1. the governor ____

2. a local district representative ____

3. a senator ____

4. an appointed trustee of a state university ____

5. the chief justice of the State Supreme Court ____

6. the speaker of the House of Representatives ____

Vote for me in 2008!

7. the lieutenant governor ____

8. a municipal court judge ____

9. the attorney general ____

10. a member of the General Assembly ____

ANSWERS: 1.B 2.A 3.A 4.B 5.C 6.A 7.B 8.C 9.B 10.A

All Around Pennsylvania! Bubblegram

Bubble up on your knowledge of Pennsylvania's bordering states and bodies of water.

Fill in the bubblegram by using the clues below.

1. A state east of Pennsylvania
2. A state south of Pennsylvania
3. A state north of Pennsylvania
4. A state southwest of Pennsylvania
5. A state west of Pennsylvania
6. A river in the western part of Pennsylvania

1. __ Ⓞ __ __ __ Ⓞ __ __
2. __ __ __ Ⓞ __ __ __ __
3. __ Ⓞ __ __ __ __ Ⓞ
4. __ __ __ Ⓞ __ __ __ __ __ __ __
5. __ __ __ Ⓞ
6. __ __ __ __ __ __ __ Ⓞ __

Now unscramble the "bubble" letters to find out the mystery word!
Hint: What is Pennsylvania's nickname?

The __ __ __ __ __ __ __ __ State!

ANSWERS: 1. New Jersey 2. Maryland 3. New York 4. West Virginia 5. Ohio 6. Allegheny
MYSTERY WORD: Keystone

Pennsylvania's Party Parks

Not only is Pennsylvania crammed with history, it also has more amusement parks than any other state in the nation! Dorney Park and Wildwater Kingdom in Allentown houses the *Steel Force* rollercoaster, which plummets 205 feet (63 meters) and then speeds through tunnels and camelback humps!

Pittsburgh is the home of Kennywood Park, one of the wildest parks in the state. Kennywood's *Steel Phantom* rollercoaster was the fastest coaster in the world when it opened in 1991. The stomach-wrenching ride cruises along at speeds up to 80 miles (129 kilometers) per hour, and drops its passengers a thrilling 225 feet (69 meters)!

Kennywood also is the home of the *Pitt Fall*, which is the tallest freefall ride in the world! This jaw-dropper plunges passengers from 251 feet (77 meters) in the air! Riders rip through the air at a screaming 100 feet (30 meters) per second! Kennywood's *Sky Coaster* hoists its riders 200 feet (60 meters) into the air, and then swings them between two tall towers! Yikes!

Using the information in the paragraphs above, graph the heights of the different Pennsylvania rides listed. The first one has been done for you.

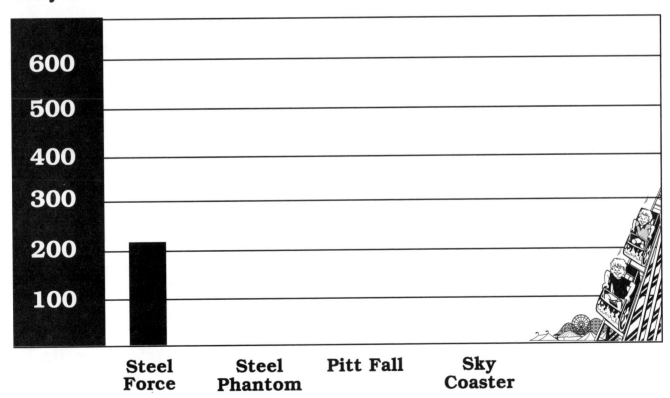

Steel Force	Steel Phantom	Pitt Fall	Sky Coaster

The Liberty Bell

When you visit Philadelphia, make sure you see the Liberty Bell! This bell is INSCRIBED with the words "Proclaim Liberty throughout the Land unto all the INHABITANTS thereof." The bell was originally CAST in England, and hung in the State House steeple in 1753. It weighed 2,080 pounds (944 kilograms)!

The first time it was rung, a huge crack MATERIALIZED in its side. The assembly ordered another bell from England, but it didn't sound right. The original bell was left in the steeple. When the British came, the Liberty Bell was hidden under the FLOORBOARDS of an Allentown church. After the bell was rehung, it cracked twice more and never rang again.

See if you can figure out the meanings of these words from the story above.

1. inscribed:_____

2. inhabitants:_____

3. cast:_____

4. materialized:_____

5. floorboards:_____

Now check your answers in a dictionary. How close did you get to the real definitions?

In the Beginning, There Was a Colony

Around 1615 and 1616, French and Dutch explorers travelled through parts of Pennsylvania. Étienne Brulé of France investigated the Susquehanna River, and Cornelius Hendricksen of Holland sailed up the Delaware River.

In 1681, William Penn of England founded the 12th of the original 13 colonies. He wished to found a Quaker settlement in the New World, and he obtained a charter from King Charles to start his colony. Penn vowed to make it a home for people of all religions.

Help William Penn find his way to Pennsylvania!

PENNSYLVANIA

Finish

Start

ENGLAND

©2003 Carole Marsh/Gallopade International/800-536-2GET/www.pennsylvaniaexperience.com/Page 11

U.S. Time Zones

Would you believe that the contiguous United States is divided into four time zones? It is! Because of the rotation of the earth, the sun travels from east to west. Whenever the sun is directly overhead, we call that time noon. When it is noon in Philadelphia, the sun has a long way to go before it is directly over San Francisco, California. When it is 12:00 p.m. (noon) in Pittsburgh, it is 11:00 a.m. in Chicago, Illinois. There is a one-hour time difference between each zone!

Look at the time zones on the map below, then answer the following questions:

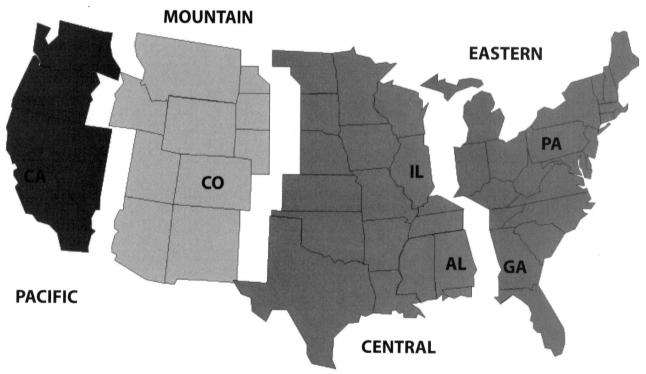

1. When it is 10:00 a.m. in Philadelphia, Pennsylvania what time is it in California? _____ a.m.

2. When it is 3:30 p.m. in Atlanta, Georgia what time is it in Pennsylvania? _____ p.m.

3. In what time zone is Pennsylvania located? _____

4. In what time zone is Colorado located? _____

5. If it is 10:00 p.m. in Harrisburg, Pennsylvania what time is it in Alabama? _____ p.m.

ANSWERS: 1. 7:00 a.m. 2. 3:30 p.m. 3. Eastern 4. Mountain 5. 9:00 p.m.

Sing Like a Pennsylvania Bird
Word Jumble!

Arrange the jumbled letters in the proper order for the names of birds found in Pennsylvania.

OSPREY

OWL

GROUSE

MEADOWLARK

BLUEBIRD

ORIOLE

ROBIN

SPARROW

WARBLER

EAGLE

L W O ___ ___ ___

O O I R L E ___ ___ ___ ___ ___ ___

N I B O R ___ ___ ___ ___ ___

G L A E E ___ ___ ___ ___ ___

K L R E D A O W M A ___ ___ ___ ___ ___ ___ ___ ___ ___

S P R R W O A ___ ___ ___ ___ ___ ___ ___

S E R O G U ___ ___ ___ ___ ___ ___

B R L W A R E ___ ___ ___ ___ ___ ___ ___

E L B B R U I D ___ ___ ___ ___ ___ ___ ___ ___

Y S P E O R ___ ___ ___ ___ ___ ___

School Rules!

By the 1990s, Pennsylvania had 65 public and 154 private colleges and universities. The University of Pennsylvania was founded in 1740 as a charity school in Philadelphia and opened its first medical college in 1765. Ben Franklin was one of the university's founders! Pennsylvania State University was founded in 1855 and now has 23 campuses around the state.

Complete the names of these Pennsylvania schools. Use the Word Bank to help you. Then, use the answers to solve the code at the bottom.

WORD

Swarthmore

Drexel

Mawr

BANK

Pittsburgh

Lehigh

Carnegie Mellon

1. __ __ __ __ __ __ University in Philadelphia

1

2. Bryn __ __ __ __ College in Bryn Mawr

6

3. __ __ __ __ __ __ University in Bethlehem

2

4. __ __ __ __ __ __ __ __ __ __ __ __ __ __ University

7   4

in Pittsburgh

5. The University of __ __ __ __ __ __ __ __ __ __ __ __

3

6. __ __ __ __ __ __ __ __ __ __ College in Swarthmore

5

The coded message tells you what all college students want.

__ __ __ __ __ __ __
1 2 3 4 5 6 7

ANSWERS: 1.Drexel 2.Mawr 3.Lehigh 4.Carnegie Mellon 5.Pittsburgh 6.Swarthmore **MESSAGE:** diploma

Let's Get Physical!

When we learn about the geography of Pennsylvania, we use special words to describe it. These words describe the things that make each part of the state interesting.

See if you can match these geographical terms with their definitions!

1. gorge
2. glacier
3. tributary
4. region
5. mound
6. lowland
7. valley
8. strait
9. mountain range
10. highland

A. a stretch of low land lying between hills or mountains

B. a deep, narrow passage between mountains

C. a pile or heap of earth

D. a narrow body of water joining two larger ones

E. an area of hills or mountains higher than the land around it

F. a river or stream that flows into a larger body of water

G. an area of land

H. a large mass of ice that moves very slowly down a mountain or across land until it melts

I. an area of land that is lower than the land around it

J. a group of mountains

ANSWERS: 1.B 2.H 3.F 4.G 5.C 6.I 7.A 8.D 9.J 10.E

©2003 Carole Marsh/Gallopade International/800-536-2GET/www.pennsylvaniaexperience.com/Page 15

It's a Pretty Pennsylvania State Flag!

Pennsylvania's state flag is deep blue, with the state seal in the center. The seal has a picture of a ship, a plow, and sheaves of wheat on a shield. A black horse is on each side, and an eagle sits on the top of the shield. Under the shield are an olive branch and a cornstalk. The current design was adopted in 1907. **Color the state flag.**

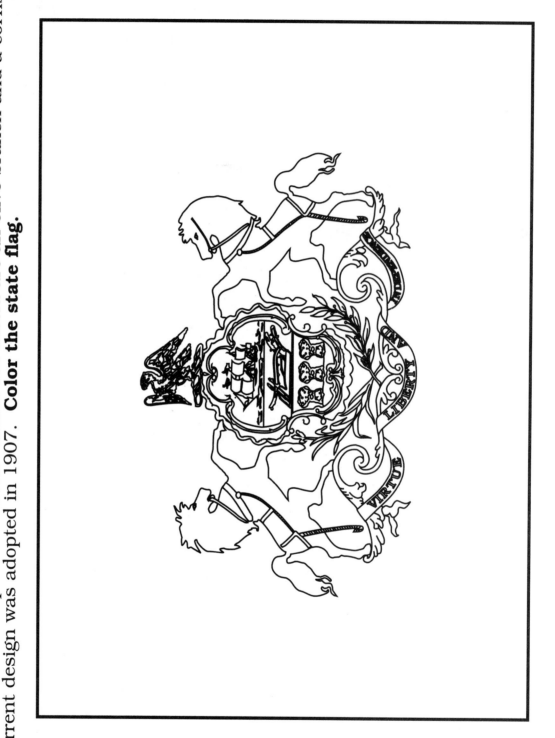

©2003 Carole Marsh/Gallopade International/800-536-2GET/www.pennsylvaniaexperience.com/Page 16

Design your own Diamante on Pennsylvania!

A *diamante* is a cool diamond-shaped poem on any subject.

You can write your very own diamante poem on pennsylvania by following the simple line by line directions below. Give it a try!

Line 1:   Write the name of your state.

Line 2:   Write the names of two animals native to your state.

Line 3:   Write the names of three of your state's important cities.

Line 4:   Write the names of four of your state's important industries or agricultural products.

Line 5:   Write the names of your state tree and state bird.

Line 6:   Write the names of two of your state's landforms.

Line 7:   Write the word that completes this sentence: Pennsylvania's nickname is the _____ State.

_____

_____   _____

_____   _____   _____

_____   _____   _____   _____

_____   _____   _____

_____   _____

_____

You're the poet.
Did you know it?

Pennsylvania, the Keystone State!

Match the name of each Pennsylvania state symbol on the left with its picture.

State Bird

State Flower

State Tree

State Dog

State Animal

State Insect

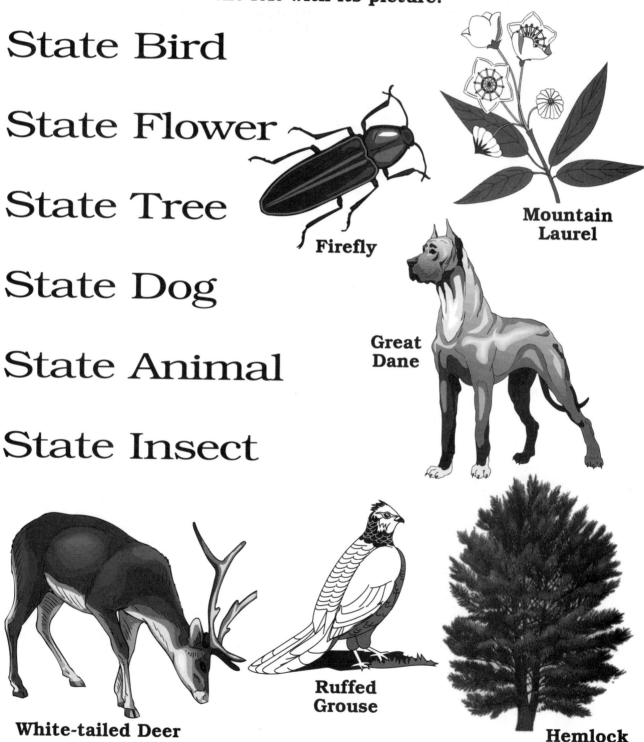

Firefly

Mountain Laurel

Great Dane

White-tailed Deer

Ruffed Grouse

Hemlock

©2003 Carole Marsh/Gallopade International/800-536-2GET/www.pennsylvaniaexperience.com/Page 18

History Mystery Tour!

Pennsylvania is busting at the seams with history! Here are just a few of the many historical sites that you might visit. Try your hand at locating them on the map! **Draw the symbol for each site on the Pennsylvania map below.**

 Bushy Run Battlefield: In 1763, Chief Pontiac led the Shawnee and Delaware Indians into a final attack near Greensburg.

 Daniel Boone Homestead: Boone was born here in 1734. It's located near Reading, and shows the lifestyles of three families during the 1700s.

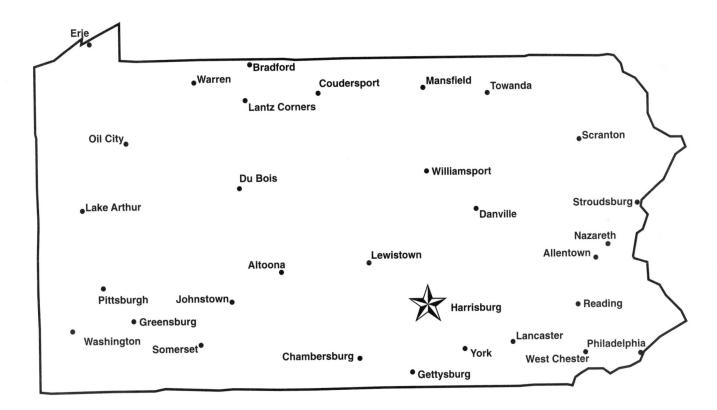

 Flagship Niagara/Erie Maritime Museum: In 1813, Commodore Oliver Hazard Perry led the *Niagara* to victory in the Battle of Lake Erie. Today, you can see the *Niagara* near Erie.

 Valley Forge National Historical Park: During the winter of 1777-1778, George Washington and his Continental Army camped at Valley Forge, northwest of Philadelphia.

Pennsylvania Places!

Use the Word Bank to help you complete the sentences below and learn about some of the exciting Pennsylvania sites you can visit!

1. Hold onto your lunch when you visit _ _ _ _ _ _ _ _ Amusement Park, the third-oldest in the United States!

2. The _ _ _ _ _ _ _ _ Mint in Media makes an incredible variety of collectibles – even a Star Trek chess set!

3. See the Cathedral of Learning at the University of _ _ _ _ _ _ _ _ _ _, the tallest education building in the world!

4. At Lake Erie, you can visit the _ _ _ _ _ _ _ Isle State Park's beautiful beaches.

5. _ _ _ _ _ _ _ _ _ _ _ _ Hall in Philadelphia was the site of the signing of the Declaration of Independence!

6. See the site of one of the battles leading to the French and Indian War at Fort _ _ _ _ _ _ _ _ _ National Battlefield.

7. In Mercer County, you can see the _ _ _ _ _ _ _ _ One-Room School Museum.

8. You can ride the _ _ _ _ _ _ _ _ _ _ Historic Railroad up to the Eagles Ironworks in Milesburg.

WORD BANK

Presque
Caldwell
Independence
Pittsburgh
Necessity
Idlewild
Bellefonte
Franklin

ANSWERS: 1.Idlewild 2.Franklin 3.Pittsburgh 4.Presque 5.Independence 6.Necessity 7.Caldwell 8.Bellefonte

The Quakers of Pennsylvania

     William Penn joined the Society of Friends (Quakers) when he was 23. The Quakers believed that worship should be simple and that violence was a sin. They also believed that all people are equal, and dressed plainly. Quakers were also abolitionists who opposed slavery.

     Unfortunately, Quakers were often persecuted for their beliefs in 17th century England. Penn wanted to find a safe, peaceful place for all Quakers to live. He finally was given a charter by King Charles II, and established his colony as a "Holy Experiment." He maintained peace with the Indians. He also named his new city after a word in Greek that means "City of Brotherly Love" – Philadelphia!

Use information from the story above to complete the crossword.

1. Penn was a member of the _____. (DOWN)
2. He founded the town of _____. (ACROSS)
3. They had a _____ relationship with the Indians. (DOWN)
4. Another name for Quakers is the _____ of Friends. (ACROSS)
5. Quakers believe that all people are _____. (DOWN)
6. "Philadelphia" means "City of Brotherly _____." (ACROSS)

ANSWERS: 1.Quakers 2.Philadelphia 3.peaceful 4.Society 5.equal 6.love

Pennsylvania Rules!

Use the code to complete the sentences.

A	B	C	D	E	F	G	H	I	J	K	L	M	N	O	P	Q	R	S	T
1	2	3	4	5	6	7	8	9	10	11	12	13	14	15	16	17	18	19	20

U	V	W	X	Y	Z
21	22	23	24	25	26

1. State rules are called ___ ___ ___ ___.
   12   1   23   19

2. Laws are made in our state ___ ___ ___ ___ ___ ___ ___.
   3   1   16   9   20   15   12

3. The leader of our state is the ___ ___ ___ ___ ___ ___ ___ ___.
   7   15   22   5   18   14   15   18

4. We live in the state of ___ ___ ___ ___ ___ ___ ___ ___ ___ ___ ___ ___.
   16   5   14   14   19   25   12   22   1   14   9   1

5. The capital of our state is ___ ___ ___ ___ ___ ___ ___ ___ ___ ___.
   8   1   18   18   9   19   2   21   18   7

P E N N S Y L V A N I A ! ! !

ANSWERS: 1.laws 2.capitol 3.governor 4.Pennsylvania 5.Harrisburg

©2003 Carole Marsh/Gallopade International/800-536-2GET/www.pennsylvaniaexperience.com/Page 22

A Rough Row to Hoe!

The people who first came to Pennsylvania were faced with a lot of hard work to survive in their new home. Although Quakers were the first to settle Pennsylvania, Anglicans moved there, too. Many German-speaking groups also moved to the area and came to be known as the Pennsylvania Dutch.

Circle the things settlers in Pennsylvania would need.

©2003 Carole Marsh/Gallopade International/800-536-2GET/www.pennsylvaniaexperience.com/Page 23

Buzzing Around Pennsylvania!

Write the answers to the questions below. To get to the beehive, follow a path through the maze.

1. Pennsylvania was the _____ state to enter the Union.

2. The first people to live in Pennsylvania were the American _____.

3. The capital of Pennsylvania is _____.

4. A body of water to the east of Pennsylvania is Lake _____.

5. The _____ River forms the eastern border of the state.

6. The largest and bloodiest battle of the Civil War took place in _____.

7. Pennsylvania is officially called a _____.

8. _____ is the largest city in Pennsylvania.

9. Pennsylvania's only national forest is the_____ National Forest.

10. Mount _____ is the highest point in Pennsylvania.

ANSWERS: 1.2nd **2.**Indians **3.**Harrisburg **4.**Erie **5.**Delaware **6.**Gettysburg **7.**commonwealth **8.**Philadelphia **9.**Allegheny **10.**Davis

©2003 Carole Marsh/Gallopade International/800-536-2GET/www.pennsylvaniaexperience.com/Page 24

Pennsylvania Through the Years!

Many great things have happened in Pennsylvania throughout its history. Chronicle the following important Pennsylvania events by solving math problems to find out the years in which they happened.

1. French explorer Etienne Brulé follows the Susquehanna River to its mouth.
    4÷4=   2x3=   5-4=   3+2=

2. New Sweden is established near Philadelphia.
    3-2=   4+2=   6÷2=   2x4=

3. William Penn arrives at Pennsylvania.
    6-5=   2+4=   5+3=   4-2=

4. Benjamin Franklin moves to Philadelphia.
    0+1=   4+3=   7-5=   6-3=

5. Pennsylvania Assembly declares "no taxation without representation!"
    6-5=   6+1=   4+2=   7+1=

6. The Constitutional Convention is held in Philadelphia.
    3÷3=   9-2=   2x4=   3+4=

7. The state capital is established at Harrisburg.
    4-3=   6+2=   3÷3=   3-1=

8. Oliver Hazard Perry defeats the British Navy in the Battle of Lake Erie.
    6÷6=   5+3=   7-6=   3+0=

9. The Battle of Gettysburg is fought from July 1 to July 3.
    4÷4=   4+4=   5+1=   6-3=

10. The first portion of the Pennsylvania Turnpike is opened.
    4-3=   2+7=   2x2=   9-9=

ANSWERS: 1.1615 2.1638 3.1682 4.1723 5.1768 6.1787 7.1812 8.1813 9.1863 10.1940

Festive Pennsylvania!

Every year, Pennsylvanians have a wide variety of festivals, fairs, and events to choose from. **See if you can match these events with the city or town in which they are held.**

1. Pennsylvania Farm Show
2. Groundhog Day Festivities
3. Cherry Blossom Festival
4. Civil War Heritage Days
5. Musikfest
6. Scottish Games and Country Fair
7. Little League Baseball World Series
8. Chrysanthemum Festival

A. Bethlehem
B. Devon
C. Kennett Square
D. Wilkes-Barre
E. Harrisburg
F. Punxsutawney
G. South Williamsport
H. Gettysburg

ANSWERS: 1.E 2.F 3.D 4.H 5.A 6.B 7.G 8.C

Rhymin' Riddles

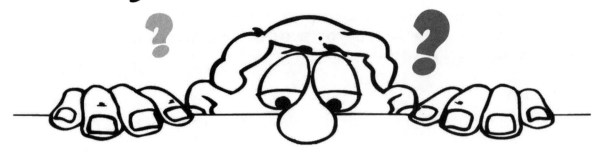

1. I am a Mid-Atlantic state, and my name starts with a "P";
   Penn and other Quakers came, looking for liberty.

Who am I? _____

2. We stretch across the land, so high and so wide;
   Along the Pennsylvania border, a beautiful sight we provide.

Who are we? _____ _____

3. I came to Gettysburg, as the president of the states;
   I wanted to speak about the war, to honor its greats.

Who am I? _____ _____

4. We lived in Pennsylvania before the explorers did roam;
   On the lands near rivers and mountains were our tribes' home.

Who are we? _____

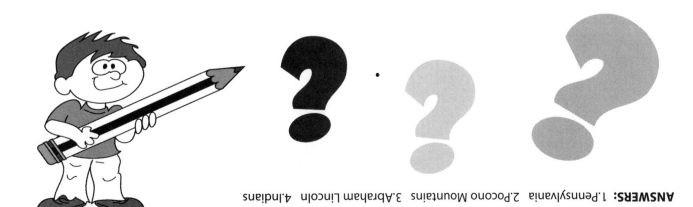

ANSWERS: 1.Pennsylvania 2.Pocono Mountains 3.Abraham Lincoln 4.Indians

©2003 Carole Marsh/Gallopade International/800-536-2GET/www.pennsylvaniaexperience.com/Page 27

Pennsylvania Goodies!

Match the name of each crop or product from Pennsylvania with the picture of that item.

corn   apples   tomatoes   eggs

potatoes   vegetables

Pennsylvania's Venomous Snakes!

Several types of snakes live in Pennsylvania, some of which are venomous (poisonous).

Using the alphabet code, see if you can figure out the venomous snakes' names.

A	B	C	D	E	F	G	H	I	J	K	L	M	N	O	P	Q	R	S	T
1	2	3	4	5	6	7	8	9	10	11	12	13	14	15	16	17	18	19	20

U	V	W	X	Y	Z
21	22	23	24	25	26

1. __ __ __ __ __ __ __ __ __ __ __
   18 1 20 20 12 5 19 14 1 11 5

2. __ __ __ __ __ __ __ __ __ __
   3 15 16 16 5 18 8 5 1 4

ANSWERS: 1. rattlesnake 2. copperhead

Historical Pennsylvania Women!

Pennsylvania has been the home of many brave and influential women.

See if you can match these women with their accomplishments. Write the letter of each lady's accomplishment next to her name.

_____ 1. Louisa May Alcott

_____ 2. Marian Anderson

_____ 3. Mary Cassatt

_____ 4. Margaret Mead

_____ 5. Gertrude Stein

_____ 6. Lucretia Mott

_____ 7. Anne Newport Royall

_____ 8. Ida Tarbell

A. Quaker minister and social reformer

B. famous 20th century author

C. author of *Little Women* and *Little Men*

D. anthropologist who studied primitive cultures

E. one of the first female newspaper editors

F. her book resulted in federal government action against Standard Oil

G. opera singer and alternate delegate to the United Nations

H. Impressionist painter

ANSWERS: 1.C 2.G 3.H 4.D 5.B 6.A 7.E 8.F

Pennsylvania Word Wheel!

Using the Word Wheel of Pennsylvania names, answer the following questions.

1. An English explorer who sailed into Delaware Bay in 1609 was Henry _____.

2. Benjamin _____ was born in Boston, but moved to Philadelphia when he was 17.

3. According to legend, the first American flag was sewn by a Philadelphia seamstress named Betsy _____.

4. The commander of the U.S. fleet at the Battle of Lake Erie was Oliver Hazard _____.

5. The Indian chief who was made a general in the British army during the War of 1812 was _____.

6. James _____, the 15th president, was born near Mercersburg.

7. President Abraham _____ gave a famous address in Gettysburg after the Civil War.

8. A Pennsylvania industrial giant who formed the Alcoa Corporation was Andrew W. _____.

9. The world famous weather forecasting groundhog named Phil can be found in _____.

10. The author of *Little Women,* Louisa May _____, was born in Germantown.

ANSWERS: 1.Hudson 2.Franklin 3.Ross 4.Perry 5.Tecumseh 6.Buchanan 7.Lincoln 8.Mellon 9.Punxsutawney 10.Alcott

©2003 Carole Marsh/Gallopade International/800-536-2GET/www.pennsylvaniaexperience.com/Page 31

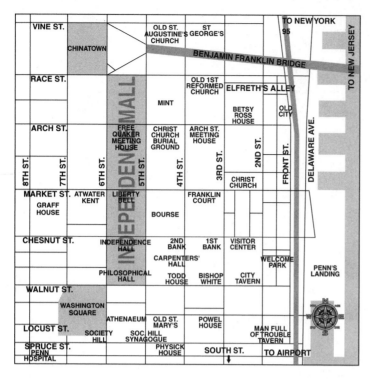

The Historic Mile Virtual Tour!

In Philadelphia, there is a one square mile (2.6 square kilometer) area that is called "America's most historic square mile." There are over 20 historical sites packed into that little area. Let's take a walking tour of the area.

We'll start out at Old St. Augustine's Church, the first home of the Augustinian monks in the United States.

1. Let's go south on 5th Street for three blocks, and then go east two blocks. We are at _____ _____, where Benjamin Franklin's house once stood.

2. Now, let's go south one block. We are at the _____ _____ of the United States, which was founded in 1791.

3. From there, let's go west one block, and south a half a block. We're at _____ Hall, which is where the First Continental Congress was held in 1774!

4. We'll go half a block north, and then a block west, to find _____ Hall, where the U.S. Constitution and other important documents were signed.

5. Finally, to finish our brief tour, let's go north a block. Here we are, at the _____ _____!

ANSWERS: 1. Franklin Court 2. First Bank 3. Carpenters' 4. Independence 5. Liberty Bell

©2003 Carole Marsh/Gallopade International/800-536-2GET/www.pennsylvaniaexperience.com/Page 32

Mixed-Up States!

Color, cut out, and paste each of Pennsylvania's six neighbors onto the map. Be sure and match the state shapes!

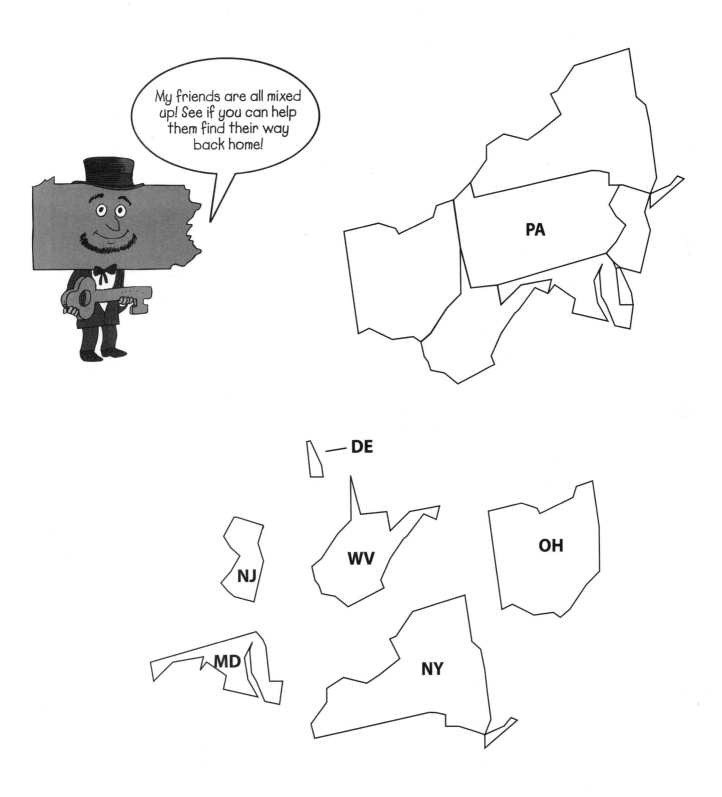

©2003 Carole Marsh/Gallopade International/800-536-2GET/www.pennsylvaniaexperience.com/Page 33

Pennsylvania People and Their Jobs!

Can you identify these people and their jobs?

Put an A by the person working on a Pennsylvania farm.
Put a B by the Philadelphia nurse.
Put a C by the Pennsylvania railroad engineer.
Put a D by the Pennsylvania coal miner.
Put an E by the photographer from the *Philadelphia Inquirer*.
Put an F by the person that works as a Pennsylvania logger.

©2003 Carole Marsh/Gallopade International/800-536-2GET/www.pennsylvaniaexperience.com/Page 34

Politics As Usual!

Our elected government officials decide how much money is going to be spent on schools, roads, public parks, and libraries. It's very important for the citizens of the state to understand what's going on in their government and how it will affect them. Below are some political words that are often used when talking about government.

MATCH EACH POLITICAL WORD WITH ITS DEFINITION.

_____ 1. Constitution

_____ 2. Governor

_____ 3. Chief Justice

_____ 4. General Assembly

_____ 5. District

_____ 6. Amendment

_____ 7. Term

_____ 8. Election

_____ 9. Veto

_____ 10. Bill

A. Number of years that an official is elected to serve

B. Lead Judge on the State Supreme Court

C. The chief executive

D. An addition to the Constitution

E. The selection, by vote, of a candidate for office

F. Pennsylvania's law-making body, made up of the House of Representatives and the Senate

G. the present version adopted in 1968, this document established Pennsylvania's state laws

H. The ability to forbid a bill or law from being passed

I. Draft of a law presented for review

J. A division of a state for the purpose of electing a representative from that division

ANSWERS: 1.G 2.C 3.B 4.F 5.J 6.D 7.A 8.E 9.H 10.I

Create Your Own State Quarter!

Look at the change in your pocket. You might notice that one of the coins has changed. The United States is minting new quarters, one for each of the fifty states. Each quarter has a design on it that says something special about one particular state. Pennsylvania's quarter was minted in 1999, and may even be in your pocket right now!

What if you had designed the Pennsylvania quarter? Draw a picture of how you would like the Pennsylvania quarter to look. Make sure you include things that are special about Pennsylvania.

Pennsylvania's Governor!

The governor is the leader of the state.

Do some research to complete this biography of the governor.

Governor's name:

_____

Paste a picture of the governor here: ➤

The governor was born in this state:

_____

The governor was born on this date:

_____

Members of the governor's family:

_____

_____

Interesting facts about the governor:

_____

_____

_____

_____

_____

_____

_____

_____

©2003 Carole Marsh/Gallopade International/800-536-2GET/www.pennsylvaniaexperience.com/Page 37

Pennsylvania Indians!

Shawnee, Delaware, Munsee, and other Indians were the first people living in Pennsylvania. They lived in the New World before the explorers and settlers came.

Circle the things that Indians might have used in their everyday life.

States All Around Code-Buster!

Decipher the code and write in the names of the states that border Pennsylvania.

A	B	C	D	E	F	G	H	I	J	K	L	M	N	O	P	Q	R

S	T	U	V	W	X	Y	Z

---

1. _ _ _ _ _ _ _

2. _ _ _ _ _ _ _ _ _

3. _ _ _ _ _ _ _ _

4. _ _ _ _ _ _ _ _ _ _ _ _ _

5. _ _ _ _

6. _ _ _ _ _ _ _ _

New York
Pennsylvania
New Jersey
Delaware
Ohio
West Virginia
Maryland

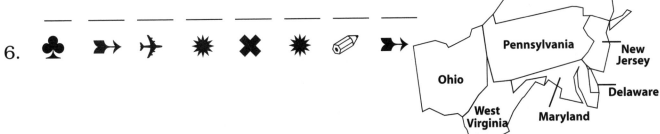

ANSWERS: 1. New York 2. New Jersey 3. Maryland 4. West Virginia 5. Ohio 6. Delaware

Peerless Pennsylvania Place Names!

Can you figure out the compound words that make up the names of these Pennsylvania cities?

ARCHBALD   _____ _____

ASHLAND   _____ _____

BALDWIN   _____ _____

BANGOR   _____ _____

BEDFORD   _____ _____

BRIDGEPORT   _____ _____

CLEARFIELD   _____ _____

EDGEWOOD   _____ _____

ELIZABETHTOWN   _____ _____

FREELAND   _____ _____

GLASSPORT   _____ _____

HOPEWELL   _____ _____

KINGSTON   _____ _____

MIDDLETOWN   _____ _____

PENBROOK   _____ _____

©2003 Carole Marsh/Gallopade International/800-536-2GET/www.pennsylvaniaexperience.com/Page 40

 # Looking For a Home!

Draw a line from the things on the left to their homes on the right!

1. Pennsylvania's governor

2. the *Niagara*

3. marker in the Soldiers' National Cemetery

4. weather forecasting groundhog

5. Siberian tigers and polar bears

6. rollercoaster enthusiast

7. wild elk

8. hikers and mountain bikers

9. Amish and Mennonite farmers

10. spelunkers

A. Punxsutawney

B. Elk County

C. Pocono Mountains

D. Penn's Cave

E. Gettysburg

F. Erie

G. Harrisburg

H. Kennywood Park

I. Pennsylvania Dutch region

J. Pittsburgh Zoo

ANSWERS: 1.G 2.F 3.E 4.A 5.J 6.H 7.B 8.C 9.I 10.D

©2003 Carole Marsh/Gallopade International/800-536-2GET/www.pennsylvaniaexperience.com/

Weather or Not!

Pennsylvania has a humid continental climate. That means that the Summers are warm, the Winters are cold, and the air is usually moist. Summers can be long and hot, especially in the southeastern part of the state. The highest temperature ever recorded was 111°F (44°C) in 1936, but the average July temperature is usually around 71°F (22°C).

The coldest Pennsylvania temperature was recorded in 1904, when it dropped to -42°F (-41°C)! Usually, Winter temperatures in January are around 27°F (-3°C). About 20 inches (51 centimeters) of snow falls every year, and Winters can be bitterly cold in the northern part of the state.

On the thermometer gauges below, color the mercury red (°F) to show the hottest temperature ever recorded in Pennsylvania. Color the mercury blue (°F) to show the coldest temperature ever recorded in Pennsylvania.

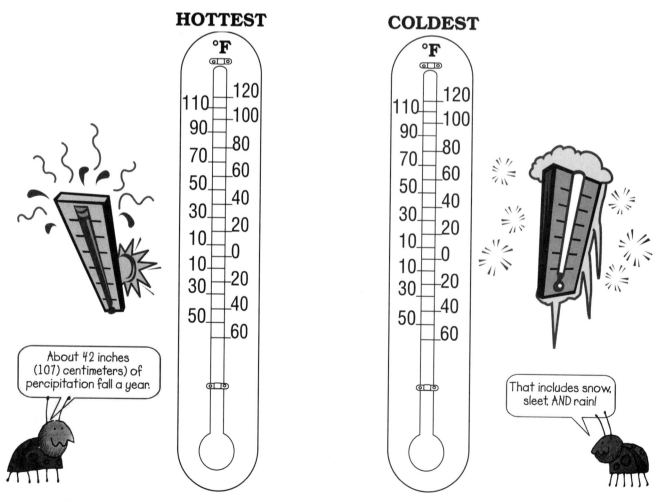

HOTTEST   COLDEST

About 42 inches (107) centimeters) of percipitation fall a year.

That includes snow, sleet, AND rain!

©2003 Carole Marsh/Gallopade International/800-536-2GET/www.pennsylvaniaexperience.com/Page 42

Something Fishy Here!

Three major river basins can be found in Pennsylvania: the Susquehanna, the Ohio, and the Delaware. Together, these three rivers drain nearly all of the land area in Pennsylvania. Many of the rivers and streams have cut spectacular gorges through mountainous and hilly regions, some of which have been used as natural passageways for highways and railroads.

Pennsylvania has more than 300 lakes, both natural and man-made. Conneaut Lake is the largest of the natural lakes. It's located in the northwestern part of the state, and covers about 1.5 square miles (3.9 square kilometers). However, the Pymatuning Reservoir is almost 26 square miles (67 square kilometers) in area!

Draw what is going on above the water line (a boat, fishermen) and add some other underwater fish friends.

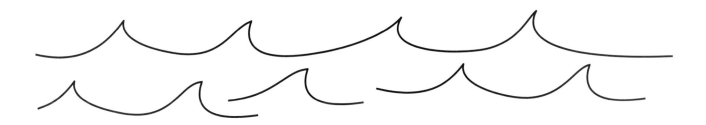

The Scenic Route!

Imagine that you are planning a field trip for your class and you're taking your classmates on a trip to some famous Pennsylvania places.

Circle these sites and cities on the map below, then number them in the order you would visit if you were traveling north to south through the state:

_____Punxsutawney

_____Ephrata

_____Altoona

_____Indiana

_____Erie

_____Philadelphia

_____Allegheny National Forest

_____Harrisburg

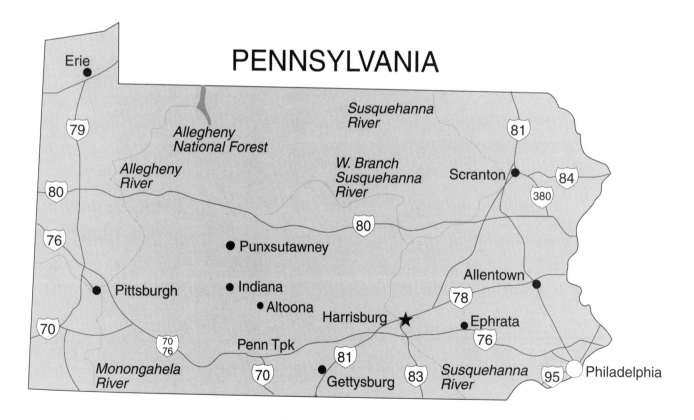

ANSWERS: 1.Erie 2.Allegheny National Forest 3.Punxsutawney 4.Indiana 5.Altoona 6.Harrisburg 7.Ephrata 8.Philadelphia

Key to a Map!

A map key, also called a map legend, shows symbols which represent different things on a map.

Match each word with a symbol for things found in the state of Pennsylvania.

airport

church

mountains

railroad

river

road

school

state capital

battle site

bird sanctuary

The First Americans

When European explorers first arrived in America, they found many Native American tribes living here.

Shawnee Indians lived in Pennsylvania in the Eastern Woodlands region of the United States. The types of homes they lived in were wigwams. **Color the Eastern Woodlands green.**

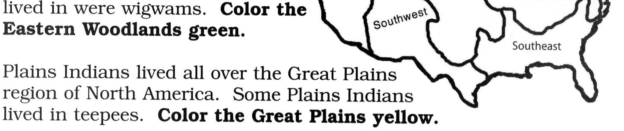

Plains Indians lived all over the Great Plains region of North America. Some Plains Indians lived in teepees. **Color the Great Plains yellow.**

Pueblo Indians lived in the Southwest region of North America. They lived in multi-story terraced buildings, called pueblos. **Color the Southwest red.**

The Five Civilized Tribes lived in the Southeast region of the United States. They lived in rectangular thatched houses called wattle and daub. **Color the Southeast blue.**

Color these houses Indians lived in. Then draw a line from the type of house to the correct region.

©2003 Carole Marsh/Gallopade International/800-536-2GET/www.pennsylvaniaexperience.com/Page 46

Pennsylvania Immigration!

People have come to Pennsylvania from many other states and countries. As time has gone by, Pennsylvania's population has grown more diverse. This means that people of different races and from different cultures and ethnic backgrounds have moved to Pennsylvania.

In the past, many immigrants came to Pennsylvania from England, Ireland, Scotland, Germany, and other European countries. Slaves migrated (involuntarily) from Africa. More recently, people have migrated to Pennsylvania from Asia and the Pacific Islands. Only a certain number of immigrants are allowed to move to America each year. Many of these immigrants eventually become U.S. citizens.

**Read each statement and decide if it's a fact or an opinion.
Write your answer on the line.**

1. Many of Pennsylvania's early immigrants came from Europe._____

2. Lots of immigrants speak a language other than English._____

3. The clothing that immigrants wear is very interesting. _____

4. Immigrants from England have a neat accent when they speak._____

5. Many immigrants will become United States citizens._____

6. Many recent immigrants come from the Pacific Islands and Asia._____

An immigrant is a person who migrates to another country in hopes of a better life.

ANSWERS: 1.Fact 2.Fact 3.Opinion 4.Opinion 5.Fact 6.Fact

Home, Sweet Home!

Match these famous Pennsylvania authors with their native or adopted hometowns.

A = Germantown   B = Atlantic   C = Bethlehem   D = Springdale
E = Allegheny   F = Shillington   G = Pottsville   H = Philadelphia

_____ 1.   **James Anderson**: Pulitzer Prize-winning playwright.

_____ 2.   **John Henry O'Hara**: author of *Butterfield 8.*

_____ 3.   **John Updike**: Pulitzer Prize-winning author of *Rabbit is Rich.*

_____ 4.   **Thomas Paine**: 18th century American author and patriot, wrote the influential pamphlet *Common Sense.*

_____ 5.   **Gertrude Stein**: developed a new writing style with minimal punctuation, and simple basic words.

_____ 6.   **Rachel Carson**: marine biologist whose book *Silent Spring* led to the banning of DDT.

_____ 7.   **Stephen Vincent Benét**: Pulitzer Prize-winning author and poet.

_____ 8.   **Louisa May Alcott**: author of *Little Women* and its sequel *Little Men.*

ANSWERS: 1.B 2.G 3.F 4.H 5.E 6.D 7.C 8.A

Pennsylvania Women and the Vote!

Before the 19th Amendment to the United States Constitution, women were unable to vote in the United States. In 1920, enough states ratified the amendment and it became the law of the land. Women gained total suffrage nationally. Women today continue to be a major force in the election process.

Match the words in the left box with their definitions in the right box.

1. Amendment	_____	A. The right to vote
2. Ratify	_____	B. A law that is an acceptable practice throughout the nation
3. Constitution	_____	C. People who could not vote in Pennsylvania until 1920
4. General Assembly	_____	D. An addition to the U.S. Constitution
5. Law of the Land	_____	E. The selection, by vote, of a candidate for office
6. Election	_____	F. To give approval
7. Suffrage	_____	G. The fundamental law of the United States that was framed in 1787 and put into effect in 1789
8. Women	_____	H. The legislature in some states of the United States

ANSWERS: 1.D 2.F 3.G 4.H 5.B 6.E 7.A 8.C

Pride of Pennsylvania!

Fill in the bubblegram with some of our state's crops and natural resources. Use the first and last letter clues to help you.

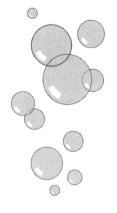

WORD BANK

VEGETABLES
WHEAT
FRUIT
LIMESTONE
CORN
OATS
COAL

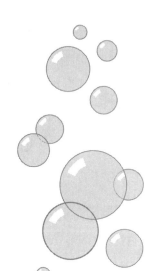

1. ___ ___ ___ L

2. C ___ ___ ___

3. ___ ___ ___ ___ ___ ___ ___ ___ S

4. O ___ ___ ___

5. L ___ ___ ___ ___ ___ ___ ___ ___

6. ___ ___ ___ ___ T

7. W ___ ___ ___ ___

Now unscramble the "bubble" letters to find out the mystery word! HINT: What is one way we can help to save our environment?

___ ___ ___ ___ ___ ___ ___ ___ ___ ___ ___ ___

MYSTERY WORD: CONSERVATION
ANSWERS: 1.COAL 2.CORN 3.VEGETABLES 4.OATS 5.LIMESTONE 6.FRUIT 7.WHEAT

Digging for Profit!

Pennsylvania is rich in mineral wealth, and has always been a major mineral-producing state. Both major types of coal, anthracite and bituminous, are found in great quantity. In fact, a region of less than 500 square miles (1,300 square kilometers) near Wilkes-Barre, Scranton, Hazelton, and Pottsville is the only place anthracite (hard) coal is found in the United States! Bituminous (soft) coal can be found all over western Pennsylvania. Other important minerals that are mined in Pennsylvania include natural gas, petroleum, and limestone. Clay, sandstone, sand, gravel, and slate are also mined there.

Put the names of these minerals found in Pennsylvania in alphabetical order by numbering them 1 to 10.

_____ sandstone

_____ limestone

_____ anthracite

_____ bituminous

_____ sand

_____ clay

_____ gravel

_____ slate

_____ natural gas

_____ petroleum

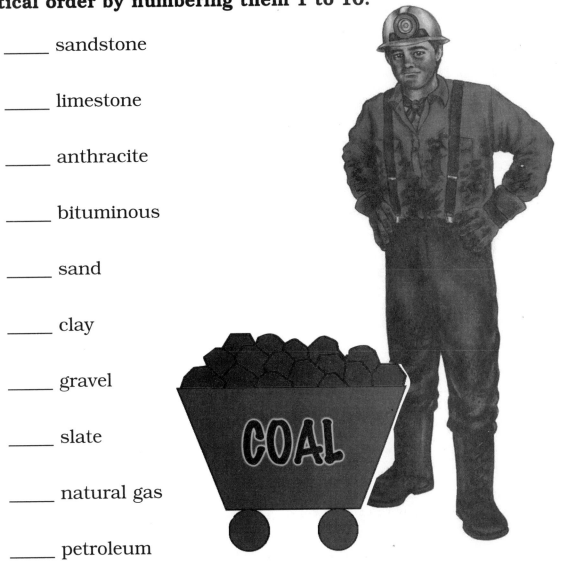

ANSWERS: 1.anthracite 2.bituminous 3.clay 4.gravel 5.limestone 6.natural gas 7.petroleum 8.sand 9.sandstone 10.slate

What a Great Idea!

1. In 1891, Whitcomb L. Judson created the first _ _ _ _ _ _ as a fastener for shoes!

2. John Behrent built the first _ _ _ _ _ in America in 1775, which he called the "pianoforte."

3. Edwin L. Drake drilled the world's first _ _ _ well in Titusville in 1859.

4. Dr. George Holtzapple first used _ _ _ _ _ _ to save a patient's life in 1885.

5. The U.S. Army needed vehicles for World War II, so the Bantam Car Company in Butler produced the world's first _ _ _ _.

6. The _ _ _ _ _ _ _ _ _ has had many "fathers," but John Fitch first built one in 1785.

oil
piano
steamboat
oxygen
zipper
jeep

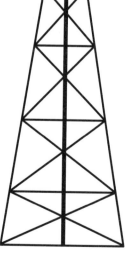

ANSWERS: 1.zipper 2.piano 3.oil 4.oxygen 5.jeep 6.steamboat

Famous Pennsylvanian Scavenger Hunt!

Here is a list of some of the famous people associated with Pennsylvania. Go on a scavenger hunt to see if you can "capture" a fact about each one. Use an encyclopedia, almanac, or other resource you might need. Happy hunting!

Samuel Barber _____

John Bartram _____

Nicholas Biddle _____

Daniel Boone _____

Andrew Carnegie _____

George Clymer _____

Stephen Foster _____

Robert Fulton _____

Stephen Girard _____

Francis Hopkinson _____

George Catlett Marshall _____

Joseph Priestly _____

Mary Roberts Rinehart _____

Betsy Ross _____

George Ross _____

Arthur St. Clair _____

Charles M. Schwab _____

Ida Tarbell _____

James Wilson _____

Andrew Wyeth _____

Haunted Carpenters' Hall

WORD BANK

Hall	stomping
ghost	odor
money	fever

Use the words from the Word Bank to fill in the blanks in the story below. Some words may be used more than once.

Carpenters' _ _ _ _ is one of the landmarks in the Historic Mile of Philadelphia. It was where the First Continental Congress was held in 1774. It also has one or more _ _ _ _ _s.

In 1798, two men robbed the bank that was located within the first two floors of Carpenters' _ _ _ _. They took a large amount of _ _ _ _ _, but were caught later when they tried to deposit the _ _ _ _ _ in the same bank! One of the men, named Cunningham, lived on the third floor of the _ _ _ _. He caught yellow _ _ _ _ _ in jail, and died soon after the robbery. It wasn't too long before people started hearing _ _ _ _ _ _ _ _ noises coming from the third floor. People kept hearing the noises every night.

In 1960 a couple moved into an apartment on the second floor of the _ _ _ _. They also heard the _ _ _ _ _ _ _ _ _ noises from the third floor, but there were no footprints in the dust on the floor there! They smelled a horrible _ _ _ _ coming from what used to be Cunningham's room. The noises and _ _ _ _ only happened at night, and the couple believed that it was the _ _ _ _ _ of Tom Cunningham.

©2003 Carole Marsh/Gallopade International/800-536-2GET/www.pennsylvaniaexperience.com/Page 54

Map of North America

This is a map of North America. Pennsylvania is one of the 50 states.

Color the state of Pennsylvania red.

Color the rest of the United States yellow. Alaska and Hawaii are part of the United States and should also be colored yellow.

Color Canada green. Color Mexico blue.

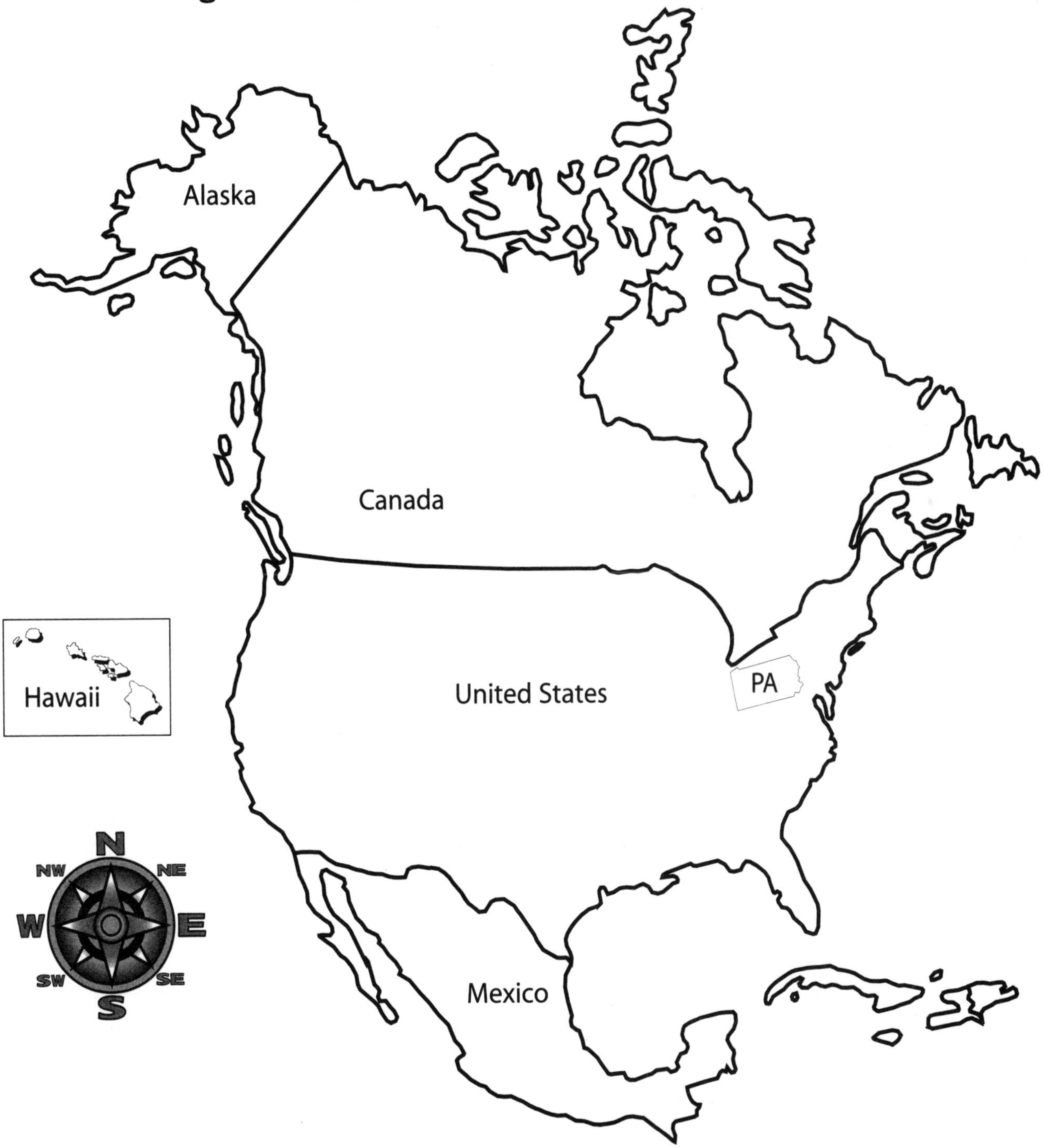

Alaska

Canada

Hawaii

United States

PA

Mexico

The Amish

A group of people have been living in Lancaster County since as early as 1727. They are the Old Order Amish. The Amish began as a branch of the Mennonite faith. Jakob Amman, a Swiss Mennonite bishop, formed his own group in 1693, and they were named after him. Unfortunately, at that time all Mennonites were being persecuted in Europe, and the Amish were too.

Many of the Amish fled to America to start a new life. Today, there are groups of Amish living in Pennsylvania, Canada, Ohio, and Indiana. They are known for their style of dress, which is plain and simple. Women wear black or dark-colored dresses, bonnets, and shawls, and the men traditionally wear hats and don't shave their beards. The Amish live mostly by farming, and many of them avoid using electricity or cars.

Read each statement and decide if it's true (T) or false (F).

1. The Amish dress in bright colors. _____

2. The Amish are farmers. _____

3. The Amish are named after Jakob Amman. _____

4. Many Amish do not use electricity or cars. _____

5. Amish men are clean-shaven. _____

6. The Amish were treated well in Europe. _____

ANSWERS: 1.F 2.T 3.T 4.T 5.F 6.F

©2003 Carole Marsh/Gallopade International/800-536-2GET/www.pennsylvaniaexperience.com/Page 56

We'll Make a Mint!

How'd you like to make some money? Philadelphia, home of one of the United States Mints, is the place to go! The Philadelphia Mint has been producing coins since the late 1700s. It's the largest mint in the world, and takes up a whole city block. The Mint has produced most of the Congressional Gold Medals awarded since 1776; bronze copies of the medals given to George Washington, John Wayne, Charles Lindbergh, and Joe Louis are still kept at the facility! Currently the Mint produces around 2 million quarters, 4.4 million dimes, 2.6 million nickels, and 20 million pennies each weekday!

For each of these money problems, figure out just how much money you have! Use the blank space to add it all up!

1.   10 quarters = _____ cents

2.   6 pennies = _____ cents

3.   2 dimes = _____ cents

4.   5 nickels = _____ cents

5.   4 dimes + 2 quarters = _____ cents

6.   3 pennies + 3 nickels + 3 dimes = _____ cents

ANSWERS: 1.250 2.6 3.20 4.25 5.90 6.48

©2003 Carole Marsh/Gallopade International/800-536-2GET/www.pennsylvaniaexperience.com/Page 57

Pennsylvania State Greats!

How many of these state greats from the great state of Pennsylvania do you know?

Use an encyclopedia, almanac, or other resource to match the following facts with the state great they describe. Hint: There are two facts for each state great!

1. president of the Bank of the United States from 1823 to 1836

2. linguist and educator

3. 15th president of the United States

4. dancer and choreographer

5. discovered several gases, including oxygen

6. wrote *The History of the Expedition Under the Command of Captains Lewis and Clark*

7. served as minister to Russia and five terms as a U.S. representative

8. described rules for any sentence in any language

9. helped to popularize modern dance

10. founder of English Unitarianism

A.   Nicholas Biddle

B.   James Buchanan

C.   Joseph Priestly

D.   Martha Graham

E.   Noam Chomsky

ANSWERS: 1.A 2.E 3.B 4.D 5.C 6.A 7.B 8.E 9.D 10.C

©2003 Carole Marsh/Gallopade International/800-536-2GET/www.pennsylvaniaexperience.com/Page 58

Pennsylvania Writers!

Fill in the missing first or last name of these famous Pennsylvania writers.

1. First name: Louisa May
   Last name: _____

2. First name: _____
   Last name: Biddle

3. First name: Benjamin
   Last name: _____

4. First name: _____
   Last name: Kaufman

5. First name: Thomas
   Last name: _____

6. First name: _____
   Last name: O'Hara

7. First name: Gertrude
   Last name: _____

8. First name: _____
   Last name: West

To be a reader or not to be a reader -- there's only one answer!

ANSWERS: 1.Alcott 2.Nicholas 3.Franklin 4.George Simon 5.Paine 6.John Henry 7.Stein 8.Benjamin

Steely Pennsylvania!

In the late 1800s and early 1900s, Andrew Carnegie founded Carnegie Steel and opened several steel plants in various cities around Pennsylvania. Steel is much stronger than plain iron and was used to make a wide range of machinery, tools, and other products. Carnegie Steel merged with several other companies to form the United States Steel Corporation in 1901, and Carnegie became incredibly wealthy. Steel production helped to make Pennsylvania prosperous until the Great Depression of the 1930s.

During the Great Depression, Pennsylvania industries (including steel) declined. Although steel production is not as high now as it was during the booming 1920s, Pennsylvania is still the top steel-producing state. Factories throughout the state manufacture a wide variety of metal products, including industrial machinery, farm implements, railroad cars, and automobile parts. Many of these products are made of steel!

Pennsylvania steel is used to make many different things. For each of these steel products, circle whether it was probably first made in the **1800s** or in the **1900s**.

1.	airplane	1800s	1900s
2.	horse-drawn plow	1800s	1900s
3.	washing machine	1800s	1900s
4.	Jeep	1800s	1900s
5.	knife and fork	1800s	1900s
6.	railroad tracks	1800s	1900s

ANSWERS: 1.1900s 2.1800s 3.1900s 4.1900s 5.1800s 6.1800s

A River Runs Through It!

RIVER BANK
Allegheny
Delaware
Juniata
Susquehanna
Monongahela
Schuylkill

The state of Pennsylvania is blessed with many rivers. See if you can wade right in and figure out which river name completes the sentences below!

1. You can find the _ _ _ _ _ _ _ _ _ _ _ River in the western part of the state.

2. The _ _ _ _ _ _ _ _ _ River actually runs along the border of Pennsylvania and New Jersey!

3. The _ _ _ _ _ _ _ _ _ _ River runs out of the National Forest of the same name.

4. The _ _ _ _ _ _ _ _ _ _ _ River runs right near Philadelphia.

5. Its name may sound like a sneeze, but the _ _ _ _ _ _ _ _ _ _ _ _ River is actually quite beautiful.

6. The _ _ _ _ _ _ _ is a western tributary of the river in number 5.

ANSWERS: 1.Monongahela 2.Delaware 3.Allegheny 4.Schuylkill 5.Susquehanna 6.Juniata

Pretty Neat Pennsylvania Trivia!

A BRIDGE OVER...
The Rockville Bridge in Harrisburg is the longest stone arch bridge in the world.

A MESSAGE FROM OUR SPONSOR...
KDKA radio in Pittsburgh produced the first commercial radio broadcast.

HOME RUN!
The first baseball stadium was built in Pittsburgh in 1909.

KA-BOOM
You can't use dynamite to catch fish in Pennsylvania

BUNDLE UP!
Punxsutawney Phil is a weather-forecasting groundhog. Every year he comes out on Groundhog Day to predict the end of winter.

NO SALE!
In Pennsylvania, it is illegal to sell motor vehicles on Sundays.

WAKE UP!
It is illegal to sleep on top of a refrigerator outdoors in Pennsylvania.

PULL 'EM UP!
In Connellsville, you can't wear your pants lower than 5 inches below your waist.

POINT AND CLICK!
Pennsylvania is the first state to list their website URL on a license plate.

Now write down another fact that you know about Pennsylvania.

_____

_____

_____

©2003 Carole Marsh/Gallopade International/800-536-2GET/www.pennsylvaniaexperience.com/Page 62

Independence Day

Circle the things you might enjoy on this special holiday.

Pretend you are signing the Declaration of Independence.

Write your signature here. You can even make it fancy!

The Declaration of Independence was signed in Independence Hall in Philadelphia!

Declaration of Independence

Time to Build an Ark!

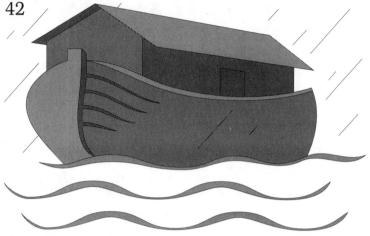

Pennsylvania receives around 42 inches (102 centimeters) of precipitation every year, including rain, sleet, and snow. Unfortunately, heavy rains can sometimes cause rivers to overflow their banks. The worst flood in Pennsylvania history happened in 1889. The South Fork Dam on the Conemaugh River burst after a period of heavy rain, and an enormous wall of water roared over the city of Johnstown. Over 2,000 people were killed by the floodwaters of 1889. In 1936, floods destroyed parts of Pittsburgh. In 1972, the Susquehanna River flooded its banks and destroyed millions of dollars in property.

Imagine that you live in an area that has had heavy rain over the past few days. You see flood warnings on your television. What should you do? Write down ways you can try to make sure you are safe during a flood.

For each of these flood survival "tips," circle whether it would be a GOOD or a BAD idea during a flood.

1. GOOD   BAD   Filling your bathtub with water early in the flood

2. GOOD   BAD   Driving your car through rising water

3. GOOD   BAD   Boiling water before drinking it

4. GOOD   BAD   Moving to higher ground

5. GOOD   BAD   Crossing water that is higher than your knees

ANSWERS: 1.GOOD 2.BAD 3.GOOD 4.GOOD 5.BAD

©2003 Carole Marsh/Gallopade International/800-536-2GET/www.pennsylvaniaexperience.com/Page 64

Pennsylvania Gazetteer!

A gazetteer is a list of places. Use the word bank to complete the names of some of these famous places in our state:

1. Sturgis _ _ _ _ _ _ _ House, the first pretzel bakery

2. Fort _ _ _ _ _ _ _ _ _, the only fort in western Pennsylvania never taken in the French and Indian War

3. The Peter J. McGovern Little _ _ _ _ _ _ Baseball Museum in Williamsport

4. The _ _ _ _ _ _ _ _ factory, home of crayons

5. _ _ _ _ _ _ Forge National Historical Park

6. The _ _ _ _ _ _ _ _ _ _ _ Coal Mine near Scranton

7. _ _ _ _ _ _ _ _ _ _ _ _ _, a house designed by Frank Lloyd Wright

8. The _ _ _ _ _ _ _ Mountains in northeast Pennsylvania

WORD BANK

Crayola	Lackawanna	League	Fallingwater
Valley	Pretzel	Endless	Ligonier

ANSWERS: 1.Pretzel 2.Ligonier 3.League 4.Crayola 5.Valley 6.Lackawanna 7.Fallingwater 8.Endless

©2003 Carole Marsh/Gallopade International/800-536-2GET/www.pennsylvaniaexperience.com/Page 65

Mixed-Up Pennsylvania!

Unscramble the words below to get the scoop on all the state symbols of Pennsylvania.

1. N N T O U I M A
   E R L U A L   _____ STATE FLOWER

2. D F F E U R
   S U E G O R   _____ STATE BIRD

3. E T A G R   N E D A   _____ STATE DOG

4. K R O O B   R T U O T   _____ STATE FISH

5. G A A R I N A   _____ STATE FLAGSHIP

6. M K C O H E L   _____ STATE TREE

7. Y F F R E L I   _____ STATE INSECT

8. L O I B T R E T I   _____ STATE FOSSIL

ANSWERS: 1.Mountain Laurel 2.Ruffed Grouse 3.Great Dane 4.Brook Trout 5.Niagara 6.Hemlock 7.Firefly 8.Trilobite

©2003 Carole Marsh/Gallopade International/800-536-2GET/www.pennsylvaniaexperience.com/Page 66

Industrious Pennsylvania!

Pennsylvania has a diverse economy that includes several industries. Some industries in the state include manufacturing, farming, and tourism. Pennsylvania grows a wide variety of crops. Pennsylvanians raise cattle, chickens, and hogs. Not only that, but Pennsylvania mines produce petroleum, natural gas, coal, and many other important minerals.

Complete the following sentences.

Without the electrical equipment, I couldn't_____
_____
_____

Without natural gas, I couldn't _____
_____
_____

Without agriculture, I couldn't _____
_____
_____

Without coal, I couldn't_____
_____
_____

Without tourism, I couldn't_____
_____
_____

Without machinery, I couldn't_____
_____
_____

©2003 Carole Marsh/Gallopade International/800-536-2GET/www.pennsylvaniaexperience.com/Page 67

Pennsylvania Timeline!

A timeline is a list of important events and the year that they happened. You can use a timeline to understand more about history. Read the timeline about Pennsylvania history, then see if you can answer the questions at the bottom.

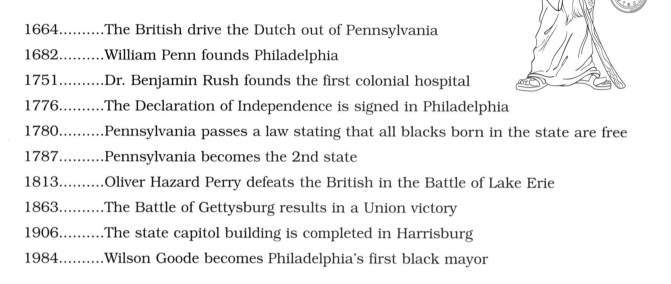

1664..........The British drive the Dutch out of Pennsylvania

1682..........William Penn founds Philadelphia

1751..........Dr. Benjamin Rush founds the first colonial hospital

1776..........The Declaration of Independence is signed in Philadelphia

1780..........Pennsylvania passes a law stating that all blacks born in the state are free

1787..........Pennsylvania becomes the 2nd state

1813..........Oliver Hazard Perry defeats the British in the Battle of Lake Erie

1863..........The Battle of Gettysburg results in a Union victory

1906..........The state capitol building is completed in Harrisburg

1984..........Wilson Goode becomes Philadelphia's first black mayor

Now put yourself back in the proper year if you were the following people.

1. If you are excited because you heard that the Declaration of Independence had been signed, the year is _____.

2. If you are happy because the area you live in just became the 2nd state, the year is _____.

3. If you are relieved to hear that the first hospital had opened in the colonies, the year is _____.

4. If you are a Union soldier thrilled with a recent victory, the year is _____.

5. If you are excited because you were going to see the new capitol building, the year is _____.

6. If you are an American naval officer feeling giddy because Commodore Perry had defeated the British, the year is _____.

7. If you are a Dutch settler who is angry because the British forced you out of your colony,   the year is _____.

8. If you are a slave overjoyed because a new law has set you free, the year is _____.

ANSWER: 1.1776 2.1787 3.1751 4.1863 5.1906 6.1813 7.1664 8.1780

I Am a Famous Person from Pennsylvania—Are You?

From the Word Bank, find my name and fill in the blank.

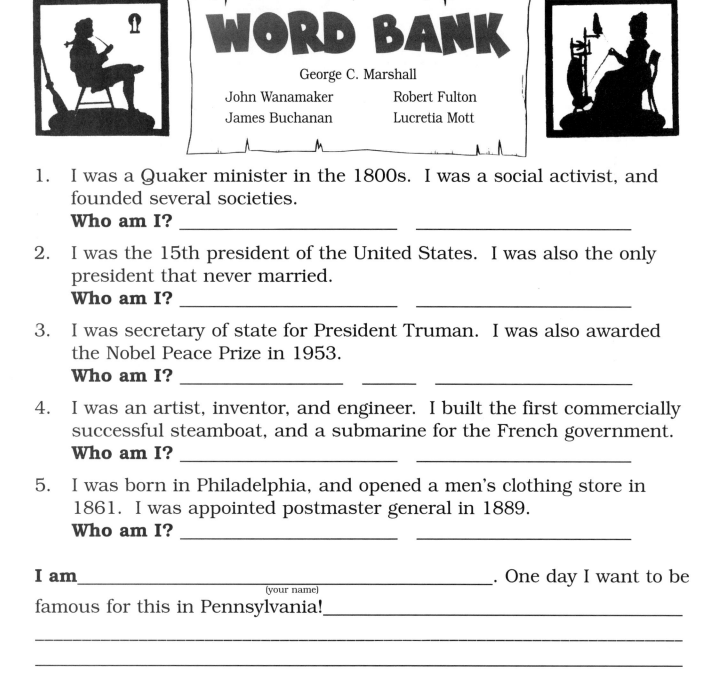

WORD BANK

George C. Marshall

John Wanamaker   Robert Fulton

James Buchanan   Lucretia Mott

1. I was a Quaker minister in the 1800s. I was a social activist, and founded several societies.
   Who am I? _____   _____

2. I was the 15th president of the United States. I was also the only president that never married.
   Who am I? _____   _____

3. I was secretary of state for President Truman. I was also awarded the Nobel Peace Prize in 1953.
   Who am I? _____   _____   _____

4. I was an artist, inventor, and engineer. I built the first commercially successful steamboat, and a submarine for the French government.
   Who am I? _____   _____

5. I was born in Philadelphia, and opened a men's clothing store in 1861. I was appointed postmaster general in 1889.
   Who am I? _____   _____

I am_____. One day I want to be
(your name)
famous for this in Pennsylvania!_____

_____

_____

ANSWERS: 1.Lucretia Mott 2.James Buchanan 3.George C. Marshall 4.Robert Fulton 5.John Wanamaker

©2003 Carole Marsh/Gallopade International/800-536-2GET/www.pennsylvaniaexperience.com/Page 69

Following Order of Battles!

Several battles have occurred on Pennsylvania soil during its history. Cut out, and arrange these battles in the proper chronological order. There's a hint for each battle.

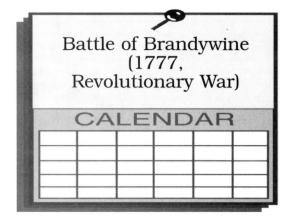
Battle of Brandywine
(1777,
Revolutionary War)
CALENDAR

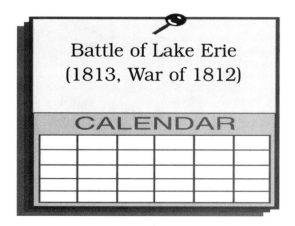
Battle of Lake Erie
(1813, War of 1812)
CALENDAR

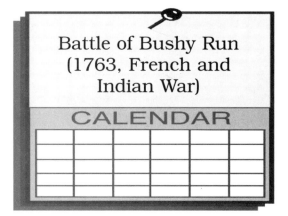
Battle of Bushy Run
(1763, French and
Indian War)
CALENDAR

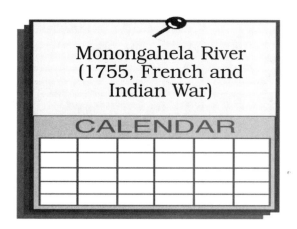
Monongahela River
(1755, French and
Indian War)
CALENDAR

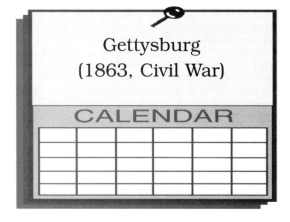
Gettysburg
(1863, Civil War)
CALENDAR

Wyoming Valley
Massacre (1778,
Revolutionary War)
CALENDAR

©2003 Carole Marsh/Gallopade International/800-536-2GET/www.pennsylvaniaexperience.com/Page 70

Indians in Pennsylvania!

When the colonists arrived in Pennsylvania, there were several Native American groups living there already. Draw a line from the group to its location on the map.

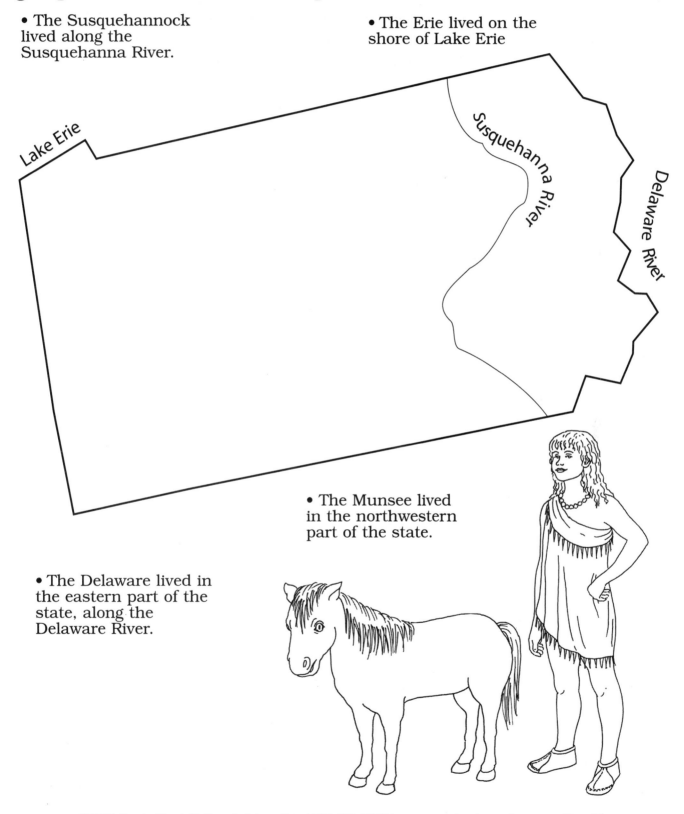

- The Susquehannock lived along the Susquehanna River.

- The Erie lived on the shore of Lake Erie

- The Munsee lived in the northwestern part of the state.

- The Delaware lived in the eastern part of the state, along the Delaware River.

©2003 Carole Marsh/Gallopade International/800-536-2GET/www.pennsylvaniaexperience.com/Page 71

Good Golly! Pennsylvania Geography Word Search!

Find the names of these Pennsylvania cities in the Word Search below:

WORD BANK

AIRVILLE	HERMITAGE	READING
ALTOONA	HERSHEY	STATE COLLEGE
GETTYSBURG	MIFFLINBURG	TITUSVILLE
HANOVER	NEW CASTLE	UNIONTOWN
HARRISBURG		YORK

```
H A R R I S B U R G I Y O R K
K F G W L B J E O X V D A B G
H E R M I T A G E H K F L U E
N E W C A S T L E A T A T N T
F T I T U S V I L L E M O I T
S T A T E C O L L E G E O O Y
F M I F F L I N B U R G N N S
C D H E R S H E Y B X L A T B
X L R E A D I N G K N C E O U
A I R V I L L E F X V I O W R
K H A N O V E R T Y L X S N G
```

©2003 Carole Marsh/Gallopade International/800-536-2GET/www.pennsylvaniaexperience.com/Page 72

How Many People in Pennsylvania?

STATE OF PENNSYLVANIA

CENSUS REPORT

Every ten years, it's time for Pennsylvanians to stand up and be counted. Since 1790, the United States has conducted a census, or count, of each of its citizens. Practice filling out a pretend census form.

Name _____ Age ☐

Place of Birth _____

Current Address _____

Does your family own or rent where you live? _____

How long have you lived in Pennsylvania? _____

How many people are in your family? _____

How many females? ☐   How many males? ☐

What are their ages? _____

How many rooms are in your house? ☐

How is your home heated? _____

How many cars does your family own? ☐

How many telephones are in your home? ☐

Is your home a farm? _____

Sounds pretty nosy, doesn't it? But a census is very important. The information is used for all kinds of purposes, including setting budgets, zoning land, determining how many schools to build, and much more. The census helps Pennsylvania leaders plan for the future needs of its citizens. Hey, that's you!!

Pennsylvania Cities

Circle Harrisburg in red. It's the state capital.

Circle Philadelphia in blue. It's where the Declaration of Independence was signed.

Circle Hershey in brown. It's where Hershey's chocolate is made.

Circle Erie in green. It's where you can see the *Niagara.*

Circle Scranton in black. It's where the Pennsylvania Anthracite Heritage Museum is located.

Add your city or town to the map if it's not here. Circle it in orange. Give it a ☺ symbol to show you live there.

Oops! The compass rose is missing its cardinal directions.

Write N, S, E, W, on the compass rose.

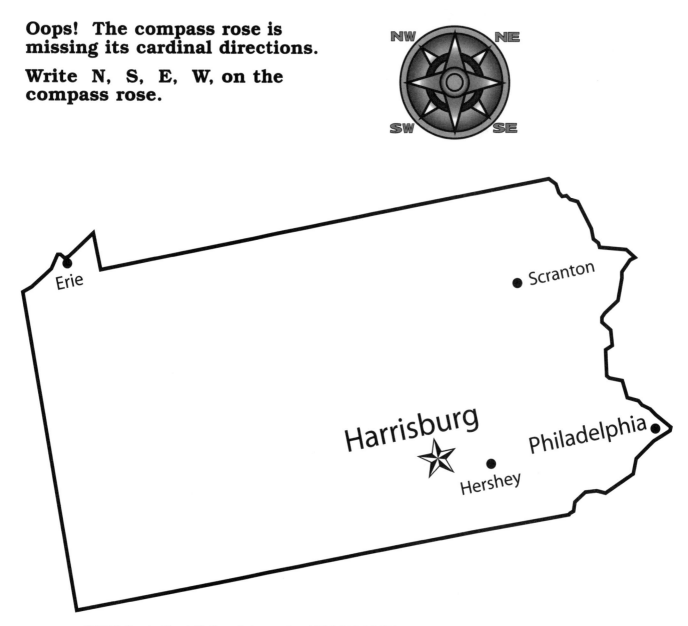

Endangered and Threatened Pennsylvania!

Each state has a list of the endangered species in their state. An animal is labeled as endangered when it is in danger of becoming extinct. Land development, changes in climate and weather, and changes in the number of predators are all factors that can cause an animal to become extinct. Today many states are passing laws to help save animals on the endangered species list.

Can you help rescue these endangered and threatened animals by filling in their names below?

1. I __ D __ __ N __   B __ __

2. D __ __ __ F   W __ __ G __   M __ S __ __ L

3. B __ __ __   E __ G __ __

4. C __ __ B __ __ E __ L

5. P __ __ __ G __ I __ E   F __ L __ __ N

6. P __ P __ __ G   P __ __ V __ __

Circle the animal that is extinct (not here anymore).

ANSWERS: 1.indiana bat 2.dwarf wedge mussel 3.bald eagle 4.clubshell 5.peregrine falcon 6.piping plover

Pennsylvania's State Song!

"Pennsylvania" was adopted as the state song in 1990. The music was written by Ronnie Bonner, and the words were written by Eddie Khoury.

"Pennsylvania"

*Pennsylvania, Pennsylvania,
Mighty is your name,
Steeped in glory and tradition,
Object of acclaim.
Where brave men fought the foe of freedom,
Tyranny decried,
'Til the bell of independence filled the countryside.*

*Chorus:
Pennsylvania, Pennsylvania,
May your future be,
filled with honor everlasting
as your history.*

1. What is mighty?

2. What do you think the word "steeped" means in the third line?

3. Whom did the brave men fight?

4. What bell do you think the song is talking about?

5. What should Pennsylvania's future be filled with?

ANSWERS: 1.Pennsylvania's name 2.full of, soaked in 3.the foe of freedom 4.Independence Bell in Philadelphia 5.honor everlasting

The Pennsylvania State Seal!

Pennsylvania's state seal is also known as its coat of arms. In the center, a shield shows a ship, a plow, and sheaves of wheat. An olive branch and a cornstalk are crossed beneath the shield, and an eagle perches on top. **Color the state seal.**

The reverse (back) side of the state seal shows a woman who represents liberty. In her left hand she holds a wand topped by the three-cornered liberty cap. In her right, she holds a drawn sword. She is trampling a lion, which stands for tyranny. The words "Both can't survive" are printed around the seal. This means that liberty and tyranny can't survive at the same time and place.

©2003 Carole Marsh/Gallopade International/800-536-2GET/www.pennsylvaniaexperience.com/Page 77

Animal Scramble!

Unscramble the names of these animals you might find in your Pennsylvania backyard.

Write the answers in the word wheel around the picture of each animal.

1. *kipchnum* Hint: She can store more than a hundred seeds in her cheeks!

2. *ethiw dleait ered* Hint: He raises the underside of his tail to signal danger!

3. *nrocoac* Hint: He has very sensitive "fingers" and uses them to find food.

4. *ntseare ttoncoliat bitbra* Hint: She would love to eat the cabbages in your garden!

5. *yarg lquiersr* Hint: He scurries around all day, burying and digging up acorns!

ANSWERS: 1. chipmunk   2. White-tailed Deer   3. raccoon   4. eastern cottontail rabbit   5. gray squirrel

©2003 Carole Marsh/Gallopade International/800-536-2GET/www.pennsylvaniaexperience.com/Page 78

A Quilt Of Many Counties!

Pennsylvania has 67 counties. Every city or town in Pennsylvania belongs to a county.

- **Label your county. Color it red.**
- **Label the counties that touch your county. Color them blue.**
- **Now color the rest of the counties.**

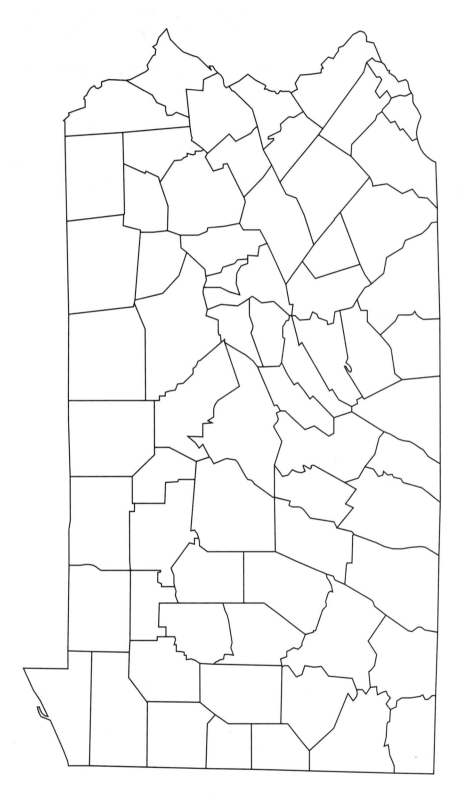

©2003 Carole Marsh/Gallopade International/800-536-2GET/www.pennsylvaniaexperience.com/Page 79

Pennsylvania Pairs!

How many of these two-name Pennsylvania places can you match? You might need a map or an atlas to help you figure them out.

1.	Beaver	A.	Square
2.	Bethel	B.	City
3.	Camp	C.	Castle
4.	Chadds	D.	Shore
5.	Dickson	E.	Hill
6.	East	F.	Carmel
7.	Forty	G.	Ford
8.	Jersey	H.	Haven
9.	Kennett	I.	Park
10.	Lock	J.	Butler
11.	Mount	K.	Falls
12.	New	L.	Fort

ANSWERS: 1.K 2.I 3.E 4.G 5.B 6.J 7.L 8.D 9.A 10.H 11.F 12.C

©2003 Carole Marsh/Gallopade International/800-536-2GET/www.pennsylvaniaexperience.com/Page 80

Contributions by State Minorities!

Pennsylvania's history is filled with the issue of civil rights, from when it was a free state before the Civil War through the 20th century. In recent decades, when many factories closed in Pennsylvania's cities, the hardest hit were often the minorities. Public housing, schools, and hospitals in the minority sections of cities like Pittsburgh and Philadelphia were in poor condition. However, many of those people became active both in city governments and within their own communities. Many African-Americans have made, and continue to make, significant contributions to the state of Pennsylvania, and the world. Below are a few.

Try matching the people with their accomplishments.

1. Sister Falaka Fattah

2. Wilson P. Goode

3. Richard Allen

4. Robert Nix

5. Herbert Arlene

6. K. Leroy Irvis

7. Henry Bass

8. Rebecca Cole

9. Daniel Hale Williams

10. Marian Anderson

A. first African-American performer at New York City's Metropolitan Opera House

B. first African-American elected to Congress from Pennsylvania

C. first black mayor of Philadelphia

D. first black speaker of the Pennsylvania House of Representatives

E. became the first black legislator in Pennsylvania in 1911

F. first African-American elected to the Pennsylvania Senate

G. founded Provident Hospital (in Chicago) in 1891

H. second African-American woman to graduate from medical school

I. created the Umoja center in Philadelphia to help teenage boys stay in school

J. born a slave, but founded and was the first bishop of the African Methodist Episcopal Church

ANSWERS: 1.I 2.C 3.J 4.B 5.F 6.D 7.E 8.H 9.G 10.A

"State Capitals"

We all know that the capital of Pennsylvania is _____ **(fill in the blank)**. Here are a few other "state capitals" that you might not have heard about.

Hershey: the "Chocolate Capital" of the United States
Reading: the "Outlet Capital" of the world
Kennett Square: the "Mushroom Capital" of the world
Indiana County: the "Christmas Tree Capital" of the world
Borough of Kane: the "Black Cherry Capital" of the world
Punxsutawney: the "Weather Capital" of the world

Write the name of your hometown here:

_____

Complete this sentence:

My hometown is the _____
Capital.

Write a few sentences describing why your town is the _____ **Capital.**

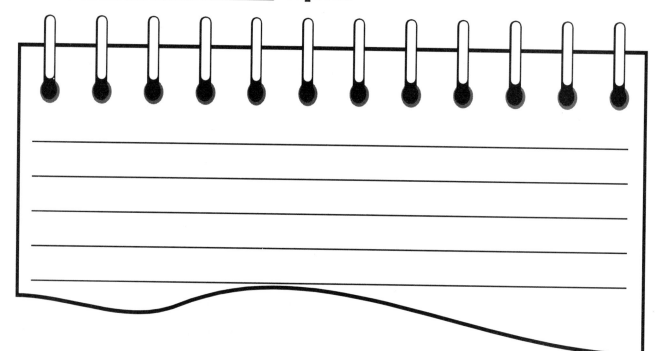

©2003 Carole Marsh/Gallopade International/800-536-2GET/www.pennsylvaniaexperience.com/Page 82

Which Founding Person Am I?

Use the Word Bank to find my name and fill in the blank.

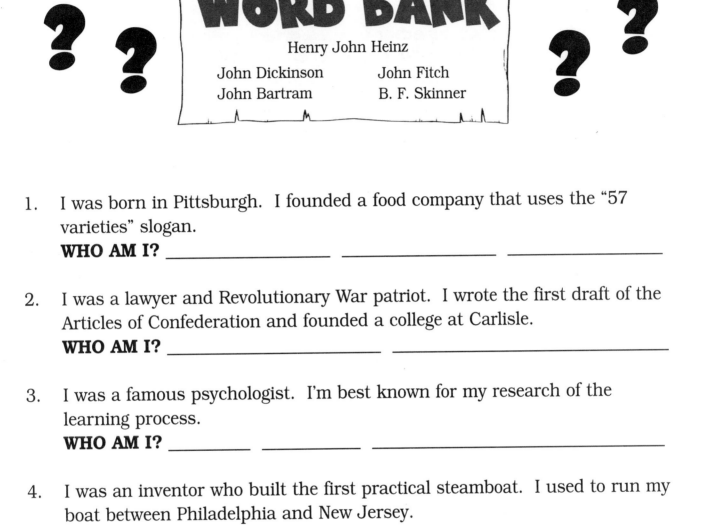

WORD BANK

Henry John Heinz

John Dickinson   John Fitch

John Bartram   B. F. Skinner

1. I was born in Pittsburgh. I founded a food company that uses the "57 varieties" slogan.
   WHO AM I? _____ _____ _____

2. I was a lawyer and Revolutionary War patriot. I wrote the first draft of the Articles of Confederation and founded a college at Carlisle.
   WHO AM I? _____ _____

3. I was a famous psychologist. I'm best known for my research of the learning process.
   WHO AM I? _____ _____ _____

4. I was an inventor who built the first practical steamboat. I used to run my boat between Philadelphia and New Jersey.
   WHO AM I? _____ _____

5. I was a botanist from Darby. I was called the "father of American botany," and I founded the first botanical garden in the colonies.
   WHO AM I? _____ _____

ANSWERS: 1. Henry John Heinz   **2.** John Dickinson   **3.** B.F. Skinner   **4.** John Fitch   **5.** John Bartram

It Could Happen - And It Did!

1776

CALENDAR

These historical events from Pennsylvania's past are all out of order.
Can you put them back together in the correct order?
(There's a great big hint at the end of each sentence.)

Hurricane Agnes blows through eastern Pennsylvania. (1972)
The British occupy Philadelphia. (1777)
Pennsylvania's first commercial railway begins operation. (1829)
Ben Franklin founds the first circulation library in the colonies. (1731)
The First Continental Congress opens in Philadelphia. (1774)
More than 2,000 people are killed in the Johnstown Flood. (1889)
The *American Weekly Mercury* begins circulation in Philadelphia. (1729)
Dutch troops from New Netherlands capture New Sweden. (1655)
Anthracite coal is discovered in the Wyoming Valley. (1762)
The first commercially successful oil well is drilled in Titusville. (1859)

1. _____

2. _____

3. _____

4. _____

5. _____

6. _____

7. _____

8. _____

9. _____

10. _____

Pennsylvania People

A state is not just towns and mountains and rivers. A state is its people! But the really important people in a state are not always famous. You may know them—they may be your mom, your dad, or your teacher. The average, everyday person is the one who helps to make the state a good state. How? By working hard, by paying taxes, by voting, and by helping Pennsylvania children grow up to be good state citizens!

Match each Pennsylvania person with their accomplishment.

1. Samuel Barber

2. Anthony Joseph Bevilacqua

3. James Buchanan

4. Alexander Calder

5. Stephen Girard

6. Alexander Haig, Jr.

7. Louis Kahn

8. Margaret Mead

A. architect and professor at Yale University

B. career army officer and White House chief of staff in 1973

C. became archbishop of Philadelphia in 1987

D. helped set up the Second Bank of the United States

E. anthropologist who studied primitive cultures

F. Philadelphia sculptor

G. first American composer whose work was performed at the Salzburg Festival

H. the 15th president of the United States

ANSWERS: 1.G 2.C 3.H 4.F 5.D 6.B 7.A 8.E

Similar State Symbols!

Pennsylvania has many symbols including a state bird, tree, dog, flag, and seal. **Circle the item in each row that is not a symbol of Pennsylvania.**

©2003 Carole Marsh/Gallopade International/800-536-2GET/www.pennsylvaniaexperience.com/Page 86

Wild Things!

The Philadelphia Zoo is the oldest in America. It was founded in 1859, and has more than 1,400 animals! There are many unusual animals there, including a pair of white lions, bi-colored tamarin monkeys from Brazil, and Madagascar giant jumping rats! Of course, there are also old favorites like bears and tigers. There is a petting zoo, and a play area called the Treehouse.

Name these animals you might find at the zoo.

Pennsylvania Products Word Wheel!

Using the Word Wheel of Pennsylvania product names, complete the sentences below.

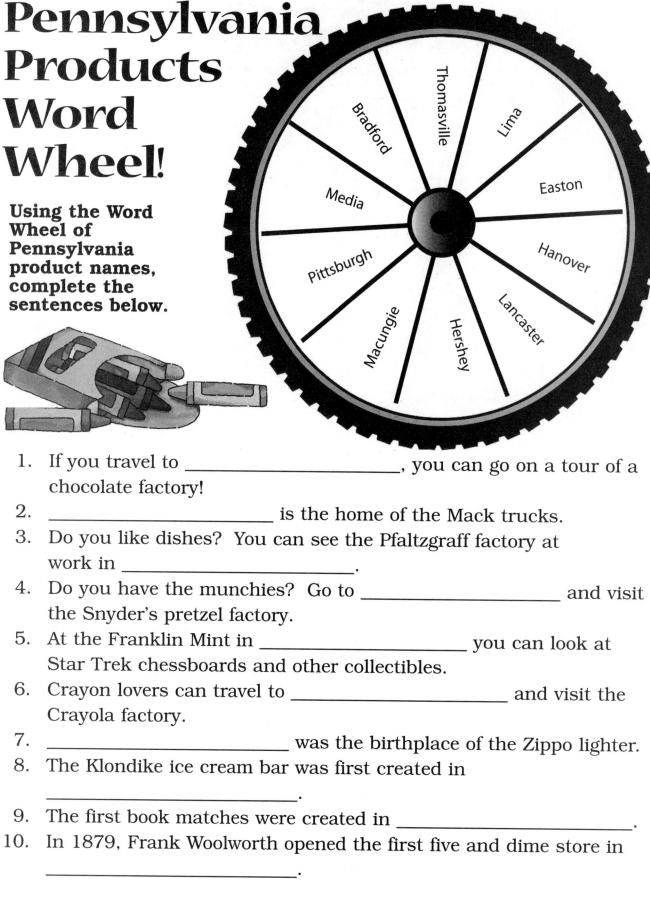

Thomasville
Bradford
Lima
Media
Easton
Pittsburgh
Hanover
Macungie
Lancaster
Hershey

1. If you travel to _____, you can go on a tour of a chocolate factory!

2. _____ is the home of the Mack trucks.

3. Do you like dishes? You can see the Pfaltzgraff factory at work in _____.

4. Do you have the munchies? Go to _____ and visit the Snyder's pretzel factory.

5. At the Franklin Mint in _____ you can look at Star Trek chessboards and other collectibles.

6. Crayon lovers can travel to _____ and visit the Crayola factory.

7. _____ was the birthplace of the Zippo lighter.

8. The Klondike ice cream bar was first created in _____.

9. The first book matches were created in _____.

10. In 1879, Frank Woolworth opened the first five and dime store in _____.

ANSWERS: 1.Hershey 2.Macungie 3.Thomasville 4.Hanover 5.Media 6.Easton 7.Bradford 8.Pittsburgh 9.Lima 10.Lancaster

# Know Your Pennsylvania Facts!

Pop quiz! It's time to test your knowledge of Pennsylvania! Try to answer all of the questions before you look at the answers.

1. Pennsylvania's state bird is the

   a. Pigeon
   b. Robin
   c. Ruffed Grouse

2. Pennsylvania became the 2nd state in

   a. 1787
   b. 1987
   c. 1687

3. The Declaration of Independence was signed in

   a. Pittsburgh
   b. Scranton
   c. Philadelphia

4. The first English colony in Pennsylvania was founded by

   a. Quakers
   b. Anglicans
   c. criminals

5. The capital city of Pennsylvania is

   a. Pittsburgh
   b. Harrisburg
   c. Philadelphia

6. Oliver Hazard Perry defeated the British in the Battle of

   a. Brushy Hill
   b. Gettysburg
   c. Lake Erie

7. The first permanent English settlement in Pennsylvania was at

   a. Harrisburg
   b. Pittsburgh
   c. Philadelphia

8. Pennsylvania's state tree is the

   a. Sugar Maple
   b. Hemlock
   c. Laurel

9. The Gettysburg Address was given by

   a. Abraham Lincoln
   b. William Penn
   c. Benjamin Franklin

10. The first American flag was sewn by

    a. Betsy Ross
    b. George Washington
    c. William Penn

ANSWERS: 1.c 2.a 3.c 4.a 5.b 6.c 7.c 8.b 9.a 10.a

©2003 Carole Marsh/Gallopade International/800-536-2GET/www.pennsylvaniaexperience.com/Page 89

Pennsylvania Battlefields!

Many Revolutionary War battles took place on Pennsylvania soil. The war finally ended in 1783 when Britain surrendered. Using the information given, find each of these battles on the map of eastern Pennsylvania below and draw a line from each to its appropriate location.

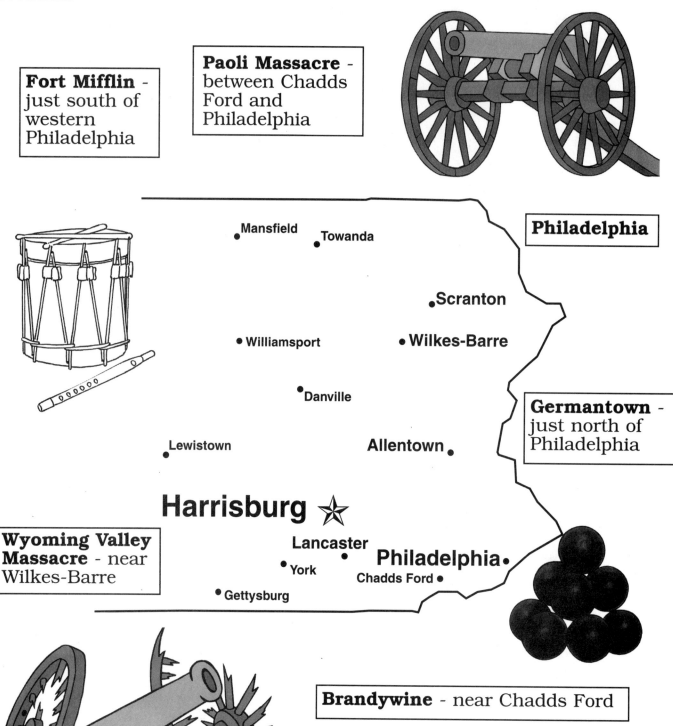

Fort Mifflin - just south of western Philadelphia

Paoli Massacre - between Chadds Ford and Philadelphia

Philadelphia

Germantown - just north of Philadelphia

Wyoming Valley Massacre - near Wilkes-Barre

Brandywine - near Chadds Ford

Mansfield · Towanda
·Scranton
· Williamsport · Wilkes-Barre
·Danville
·Lewistown · Allentown·
Harrisburg ☆
Lancaster
·York · **Philadelphia**·
Chadds Ford ·
· Gettysburg

©2003 Carole Marsh/Gallopade International/800-536-2GET/www.pennsylvaniaexperience.com/Page 90

Shoofly Pie

Shoofly pie is a delicious dessert with a crumbly filling. In the olden days, when people put it on the windowsill to let it cool, they had to shoo the flies away from it, it was so yummy! Here is a basic recipe for shoofly pie. Make sure you get an adult to help you.

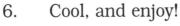

Ingredients:

1. 1 and 1/3 cups sifted flour
2. 3/4 cup dark brown sugar
3. 1/2 teaspoon salt
4. 1/3 cup margarine
5. 1 teaspoon baking soda
6. 1 cup boiling water
7. 1 cup molasses
8. 1 egg, beaten
9. 1 unbaked 9-inch (23-centimeter) pie crust
10. 1/4 teaspoon cinnamon

Directions:

1. Sift the flour, sugar, and salt together.
2. Cut in the margarine and mix until crumbly.
3. Stir baking soda into the water, then stir in the molasses and egg.
4. Pour the liquid into the pie shell, and then crumble the other ingredients over the top. Sprinkle with cinnamon.
5. Bake at 400°F (204°C) for 15 minutes, and then 350°F (177 °C) for 30 minutes.
6. Cool, and enjoy!

The Nifty Niagara!

The ship *Niagara* is Pennsylvania's flagship, and was used by Oliver Hazard Perry to defeat the British in 1813. It's been restored and is docked near Erie, Pennsylvania. You can visit this historic ship and learn about maritime life and the War of 1812.

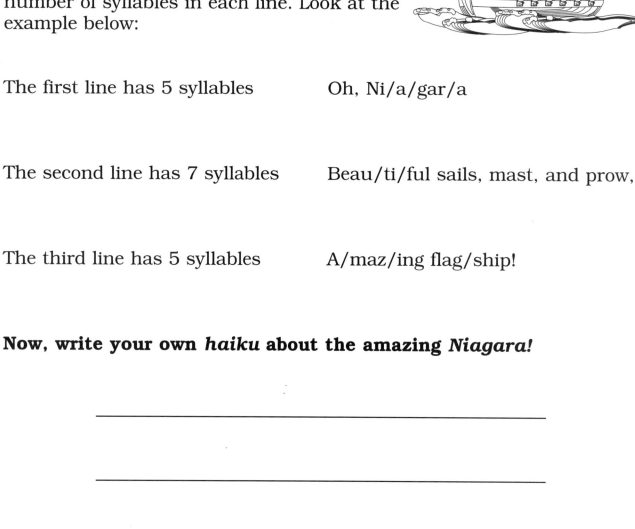

A *haiku* is a three line poem with a certain number of syllables in each line. Look at the example below:

The first line has 5 syllables   Oh, Ni/a/gar/a

The second line has 7 syllables   Beau/ti/ful sails, mast, and prow,

The third line has 5 syllables   A/maz/ing flag/ship!

Now, write your own *haiku* about the amazing *Niagara!*

_____

_____

_____

Park It!

Pennsylvania has made a real effort to preserve many of the natural habitats around the state. Several state parks and forests can be found throughout the area, and a couple of national sites too. Each is designed to help preserve certain types of animals, plants, and environments.

Unscramble the names of these Pennsylvania state and national forests and parks.

1. L E L H G A E N Y _____
   National Forest

2. U S S E Q H U N A N A _____
   State Forest

3. A N A N W A K C L A _____
   State Park

4. L E Y L A V   R G E O F _____ _____
   National Historical Park

5. S D O L W R   N E D _____ _____
   State Park

6. W A R L E D E A   A T E R W   P G A _____

   _____ _____

   National Recreational Area

ANSWERS: 1.Allegheny 2.Susquehanna 3.Lackawanna 4.Valley Forge 5.Worlds End 6.Delaware Gap

Prime Pennsylvania!

Pennsylvania is the 33rd largest state in the U.S. It has an area of 46,059 square miles (119,284 square kilometers).

Can you answer the following questions?

1. How many states are there in the United States?

____

2. This many states are smaller than our state:

____

3. This many states are larger than our state:

____

4. One mile = 5,280 ____ ____ ____ ____

HINT: 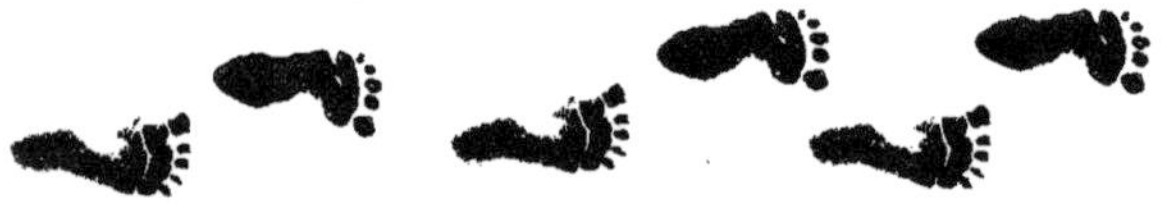

5. Draw a "square foot" here:

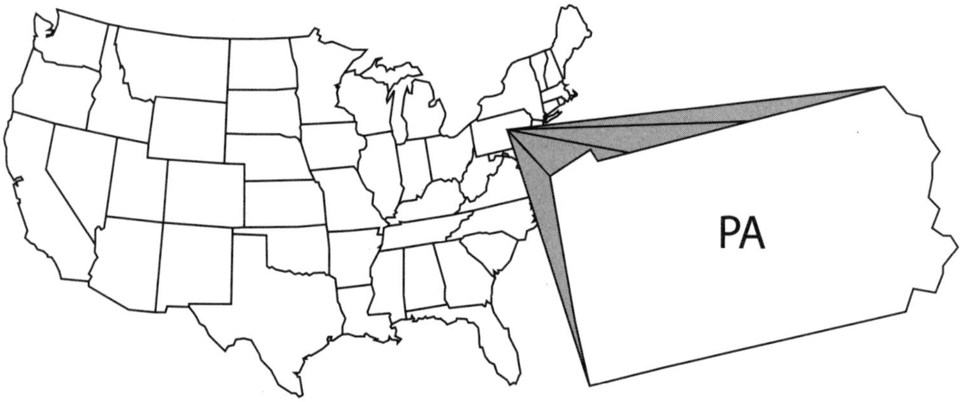

ANSWERS: 1. 50 2. 17 3. 32 4. feet 5. □

Pennsylvania Pits!

Pennsylvania has more than 1,000 caves! Nine of these caves are open to visitors. Laurel Caverns is the largest show cave. It's near Uniontown. You can see incredible towering natural limestone sculptures. Lincoln Caverns in Huntingdon is the second-largest cave in Pennsylvania there. Visitors can tour the beautiful, glittering crystal caverns. It's a spelunker's paradise!

Pretend that you are a "spelunker" (person who explores caves). What sort of tools do you think you'd need to thoroughly investigate a cave? Circle the tools you'd need below.

P is for Pennsylvania

P is for Philadelphia.

E is for eating Hershey's chocolate.

N is for never giving up the fight for independence.

N is for the new state quarter.

S is for Susquehanna.

Y is for your rich history.

L is for the Liberty Bell.

V is for victory time and again.

A is for Altoona.

N is for needing a winter coat.

I is for Independence Hall.

A is for all that the state has to offer.

Now see if you can make up your own acrostic poem describing your city or town. Be sure to use words that best describe what sets your town apart from all the others in Pennsylvania.

©2003 Carole Marsh/Gallopade International/800-536-2GET/www.pennsylvaniaexperience.com/Page 96